INTERNATIONAL STANDARD

RICHARDS REFEREN

"COLLECTORS
TREASURY and BANK OF ENGLAND
11th edition - 2001

R. J. MARLES © Original 1985

SECTION ONE
TREASURY NOTES from 1914 to 1927
(Pages 4 to 17)

SECTION TWO
BANK OF ENGLAND NOTES from 1694 to 1928
(Pages 19 to 24)

SECTION THREE
BANK OF ENGLAND - The Modern Series - from 1928
(Page 25 onwards)

FULL INDEX · BACK COVER

The Bank of England owns the copyright in its notes. Reproductions of those notes appear in this book only following authorisation by The Bank.

A compilation of averaged selling-prices drawn from dealers' lists, auctions and notaphily magazines by: R. J. Marles - with a lot of help from his friends - for

ROTOGRAPHIC PUBLICATIONS - 37 St. Efrides Road
Torquay - TQ2 5SG - England

ACKNOWLEDGEMENTS

Thanks are due to several banknote enthusiasts, both collectors and dealers. Among them are those whose lists have formed part of the pricing "policy" (an averaging of values as a guide) and, for this edition, they are:

D. G. Barney · Coincraft · Corbitt's · C. & R. Dennett · R. Flashman
B. Frank & Son · K. Goulborn · R. Jeffrey · Jak Leonard · D. Mason
P. Morris · Colin Narbeth · Notability · Michael O'Grady · Phillips Son & Neale
Spink & Son · Taunton Stamp Shop · Pam West · George White (Rose and Jane)

Terms Used To Aid Identification

The words obverse and reverse, although quite 'proper', have been eschewed in favour of front and back to distinguish one side of the note from the other. As required by The Bank of England, illustrations are no greater than half-linear size. The actual size of the note referred to is given both in inches and millimetres.

Serial Prefix Combinations

LNN means letter-number-number e.g. A12
NNL means number-number-letter e.g. 12A
LLNN means letter-letter-number-number e.g. AB12
LNNL means letter-number-number-letter e.g. A12B
L/N means letter-over-number e.g. $\frac{A}{1}$
L2/N = letter-plus-small-indicated-number-over-number e.g. $\frac{L2}{1}$

Other combinations, should they occur, will be, hopefully, obvious.

Also distinguish N$\underset{\cdot}{o}$ (dot) and N$\underset{-}{o}$ (dash)

A 'RADAR' number reads the same backwards as forwards

GRADING · PAGE 93   FULL INDEX · BACK COVER

Following 'constructive criticism', from collectors, almost all the pictures of rare notes, which we started out with, have been replaced by examples of readily available notes from "ORDINARY" collections either bought or borrowed.

Each banknote reproduction is, as required by the Bank of England, half-linear (quarter area) in size. For this edition the word SPECIMEN is required on notes from, and including Series 'C'.

PREFACE

Treasury notes are dealt with first in spite of the fact that Bank of England notes appeared some two hundred years earlier. Treasury notes were issued for a specific purpose and have a precise starting point and, more importantly for reference book purposes, a finishing point. They are complete; whereas Bank of England notes will, presumably, continue for many years and will keep requiring additional space. Even the welcomed/dreaded Euro, hopefully, will have some evidence of
BRITISH SOVEREIGNTY.

SECTION ONE
TREASURY NOTES 1914 to 1928

The Chancellor of the day, Lloyd George, just a few hours after the midnight Declaration of War, touched on the need to preserve the country's gold. The issue of notes for one pound and for ten shillings were to circulate *"As fully as sovereigns and half-sovereigns are current and shall be legal tender in the United Kingdom for the payment of any amount"*

Why not the Bank of England, with all its experience and expertise? The Bank felt that large numbers of low-value notes wouldn't be "safe" unless they were printed on special, hand-made paper. This meant a relatively slow output. The Chancellor wanted them NOW. His announcement in Parliament was on August 5th; Waterlow Brothers and and Layton provided the first of the new one pound notes on August 7th! Obviously, there must have been earlier discussions and preparations for such a speedy result. Possibly, a very fine Crystal Ball "revealed" the inevitability of The Great War of 1914/18.

TREASURY NOTES 1914 to 1928
An astonishing achievement, carried out over a single week-end, saw the printing of a vast number of the new notes. They were printed on ungummed postage stamp paper and carried the G.R. cypher watermark. Bearing the signature of the SECRETARY TO THE TREASURY *John Bradbury* the pound notes were printed in black and, appearing just one week later, the ten shilling notes were in red. Both notes were the same size and were printed on only one side of the paper. It was advisable to have all your notes face upwards before counting. Many found face down, it is said, were thrown away as scrap paper! Thomas De La Rue and Company assisted Waterlow Brothers and Layton to produce the ten shilling note. Almost at once, a second series was devised. This time banknote paper was used and a much more elaborate watermark incorporated: the Royal Cypher, value, rose, thistle, shamrock, and daffodil. Still on one side only and in the same colours, some sorting assistance was provided by varying the sizes, a little, between the two values. Included in this second series is the issue of: *THE DARDENELLES CAMPAIGN Overprints* (pages 8, 9 and 14). Third issue "Bradburys", chiefly in brown (£1) and green (10/-) speedily followed. Both sides were printed and the "typical" British banknote was established. The original purpose of the Treasury note was to gather in the gold. So successful was the exercise that silver was targetted and notes were prepared for five shillings (5/-), half-a-crown (2/6d), and even one shilling (1/-). Fear of runaway inflation through notes unbacked by real assets lead to the destruction of most of these.

4 H. M. TREASURY NOTES

No.	Date	Signature	Fine	V. F.	E.F.	Unc.

ONE SHILLING
Central vignette H. M. King George V · Green, brown, white · 4 1/8 x 2 5/8 · 104mm x 66mm

RT1 1918 (Nov.) John Bradbury:
                  A/1 (probably A/1 No. 000000 only)   - - -

RT2 1919 (Nov.) N. F. Warren-Fisher:
     L/N   B/- (only)   - - -   £3600   - - -   - - -

HALF-CROWN (two shillings and sixpence)
Central vignette of H. M. King George V   Olive-green, chocolate and white

RT3 1918 (Nov.)   John Bradbury:
     L/N   A/1 No. 000000   £4500   - - -   - - -
★   (at auction 1996) Five Colour Trials   - - -   £24,000
RT4 1919 (Nov.)   N. F. Warren-Fisher:
     L/N   A/-   - - -   £3800   - - -   - - -

(Not, officially, issued)

FIVE SHILLINGS
Central vignette of H. M. King George V · Violet, green and white · 5 x 3 · 127mm x 76mm

RT5 1917 (Dec.)   John Bradbury:
     L/N   A/-   - - -   £3300   - - -   - - -
RT6 1919 (Nov.)   N. F. Warren-Fisher:
     L/N   B/-   - - -   £3000   - - -   - - -

RT2   RT4

RT6

H. M. TREASURY NOTES
(Emergency) TEN SHILLINGS

5

Small vignette at left - very large value at right
Red and white • one side only on stamp paper • 5" x 2½" • 127mm x 63.5mm

No.	Date	Signature	Fine	V.F.	E.F.	About Uncirc.
	1914 (Aug)	**John Bradbury:**				
RT7	L/N № 6 digits					
		S/-; T/-;	---	£300	£600	£900
	(noted 1999)	T/------	---	---	"abt.UNC"	£875
	(noted 2001)		---	---	"E.F."	£750	----
RT8	№ L/N 6 digits					
		A/1	£150	£300	£500	£750
		A/-	£125	£225	£300	£500
	(noted 2001)	A/3	£125	"E.F."	£325	----
	(noted 1998)	A/4 161514	----	----	"abt. UNC"	£450
	(noted 1999)		"abt.VF"	£150	----	----
	(noted 1999)		----	----	" UNC"	£600
	(noted 2001)	A/11	----	"E.F."	£325	----
RT8a	Variety has no space between prefix and serial (see picture)					
	(noted 1996)	A/15	----	"abt.EF"	£295	----
	(noted 1998)	A/15	"no space E.F.+"		£350	----
RT9	L/N № 5 digits (A, not all letters, to Z)					
			£150	£400	£600	£950
	(noted 2001)	A/------	"V.F."	£425	£400	----
	(noted 2001)		----	"gd. E.F."	£700	----

RT7

RT8a

H. M. TREASURY NOTES
TEN SHILLINGS
UNITED KINGDOM OF GREAT BRITAIN AND IRELAND

Red & white • 5³/₈" x 3" • 136mm x 76mm
Printed only on one side
Watermark of wavy lines, Royal Cypher and British Emblems

No.	Date	Signature	Fine	V.F.	E.F.	About Uncirc.
	1915	**John Bradbury:**				
RT10	L/N plus 5 digits		£50	£100	£225	£350
	(noted 1999)		"Fine+"	£85	----	----
	(noted 2001)		----	"gd.E.F."	£250	----
	(noted 2001)	J/76	----	"E.F."	£330	----
RT11	L1/N plus 5 digits		£35	£85	£225	£300
	(noted 1998)		£45	"goodFine"	----	----
	(noted 2000)		----	"E.F."	£240	----
	(noted 2001)	A1/1	"abtV.F."	£60	---	----

RT10

RT11

H. M. TREASURY NOTES

TEN SHILLINGS
UNITED KINGDOM OF GREAT BRITAIN AND IRELAND

Red & white • 5³/₈" x 3" • 136mm x 76mm
Printed only on one side
Watermark of wavy lines, Royal Cypher and British Emblems

No.	Date	Signature		Fine	V.F.	E.F.	About Uncirc.
	1915	**John Bradbury:**					
RT12	L2/N	A2; B2; C2; +5 digits		£45	£110	£250	£350
	(noted 2000)	A2/ - -		"gdVF"	£145	- - - -	- - - -
	(noted 2000)	B2/81		- - -	"EF"	£260	- - - -
	(noted 2000)	C2/13		"gdVF"	£140	- - - -	- - - -
RT13	L/N	plus 6 digits (N to Z)		£40	£95	£260	£350
	(noted 1998)			- - -	"EF"	£250	- - - -
RT14	L1/N	plus 6 digits (P1 to Z1)		£40	£95	£260	£350
	(noted 1999) :						
	S1/62	hand-signed by Versailles Treaty signatorys				"torn"	£880
	(Flashman 2000) "Rounded Shamrock W/mk "V.F."					£500 (see RT23b)	

RT12

RT14

H. M. TREASURY NOTES
"260 DAYS"

Under General Sir Ian Hamilton, a force of 30,000 men set sail from Lemnos with the intention of making a landing on the Peninsula of Gallipoli. First ashore, 25th April 1915, were the combined contingents from Australia and New Zealand: the ANZACS. The place of their landing has since been known as Anzac Cove. Getting ashore was, relatively, easy but holding the cove in the face of brave and very tough Turkish soldiers, led by Mustafa Kemal (later called Ataturk) brought out the best in the Anzacs who achieved, probably, the only success in a disastrous campaign.

At the tip of the peninsula was Cape Helles. Cape HELL suffices to pinpoint slaughter on a vast scale. Hour after hour the British infantry scrambled down the gang-planks leading from doors cut in the side of the "River Clyde". Most were killed before they even touched the shore. Red ripples washed on to "V" beach. At "W" beach, the 1st Lancashire Fusiliers won their historic "six Victoria Crosses before breakfast" and established a toe-hold at the cost of half their number.

Fierce counter attacks by the Turks eventually reduced all Allied positions to little more than the space they physically occupied. The great Dardanelles Expedition: which was intended to relieve the static, murderous trench warfare of France, itself became the very worst kind of trench warfare where the opposing sides were so close together that hand grenades were tossed from one to the other and, often, back again before exploding. The Turks, by digging their trenches so close to their enemy, avoided being shelled by the British fleet. Attacks by the Allies couldn't push back the Turks; massive counter attacks, with huge casualties, couldn't dislodge the Allies. Gallipoli was a disaster.

On the morning of 20th December, the Turks, at first with nervous suspicion, were astonished to find that the entire Anzac force had gone. On the 9th January, the British forces at Cape Helles also "disappeared" in the same way: stealthily, during the night. Both withdrawals were brilliantly carried out without casualties.

Dardanelles
Campaign
Overprint

RT15

H. M. TREASURY NOTES   9
DARDANELLES CAMPAIGN OVERPRINT TEN SHILLINGS

No.			Fine	V.F.	E.F.	About Uncirc.
RT15	L/N plus 6 digits (AS RT13)	(Duggleby T15 · Pick Turkey PM1)				
	Y/N and Z/N		£250	£400	£650	----
	(Narbeth 1998) Z/2		"F/VF"	£495	----	----
	(noted 1999) Z/19		£350	"Fine+"	----	----
	(West 2000) Y/2-		£320	"Fine"	----	----
	(Goulborn '98)		£95 "faded, spotty + horrid"			----
	(Goulborn 2000)		"gdVF"	£425	----	----
	(noted 2001)		----	----	£900	----
	(Flashman 2000)		"gdVF"	£395	----	----

TEN SHILLINGS
Green, purple, brown, white • 5½" x 3⅛" • 138mm x 78mm
Watermark: Royal Cypher - TEN SHILLINGS - four emblems

No.	Date	Signature		Fine	V.F.	E.F.	About Uncirc.
	1918 (Oct)	**John Bradbury:**					
RT16	L/N Nº (black)	A/N		----	£140	£275	£500
	(noted 2001)	A/8		"V.F."	£105	"abt. Unc"	£495
	(noted 2001	A/19		"gd.V.F."	£165	----	----
RT17	L/N Nº (black)	A/N		£75	£140	£275	£450
	(noted 1999)	A/--		----	----	"abt. Unc"	£500
	(noted 1999)	A/3		"gdVF+"	£160	----	----
	(noted 2000)			----	"gd.E.F."	£350	----
RT18	L/N Nº (red)	B/N, C/N		£85	£450	£950	----
	(sundry 1999)			£80	£460	£930	----
RT19	L/N Nº (red)	B/N, C/N		£85	£125	£250	£325
	(sundry 2000)	B/N		£85	----	£275	£350
	(noted 2000)	B/22		----	----	"Unc"	£550

(dash · black)
RT17

H. M. TREASURY NOTES
TEN SHILLINGS

Green, purple, brown, white • 5½" x 3⅛" • 138mm x 78mm
Watermark: Royal Cypher - TEN SHILLINGS - four emblems

No.	Date	Signature	Fine	V.F.	E.F.	About Uncirc.
	1919 (Sep)	**N.F. Warren-Fisher:**				
RT20	L/N N° (red)					
		D/N	£35	£60	£125	£195
		E/N, F/N, G/N		£60	£125	£195
		H/N		£60	£125	£195
	(noted 1999)	H/30	---	"VF plus"	£125	----
RT21	L/N N̲o̲ (red)					
		D/N	£20	£50	£165	£250
		E/N, F/N, G/N	---	£40	£120	£200
		H/N	£20	£50	£165	£250
	(sundry 1998)		---	£40	£140	£225
RT22	L/N "No." omitted (J/- to S/-)					
	(sundry 2000)	J/-	£20	£60	£75	£110
	(noted 1998)	J/-	---	"gd.EF"	£95	----
	(noted 1999)	K/15	---	"E.F."	£130	----
	(noted 2000)	N/20	"gd.V.F."	£175	"Consecutive pair"	
	(noted 2000)	P/88	---	"E.F."	£75	----
	(noted 1998)	S/8	"V.F."	£85	----	----

RT21 dash · red

RT20 dot · red

H. M. TREASURY NOTES
TEN SHILLINGS
Now reads 'UNITED KINGDOM OF GREAT BRITAIN AND NORTHERN IRELAND'

No.	Date	Signature	Fine	V.F.	E.F.	About Uncirc.
	1927 (July)	**N. F. Warren-Fisher:**				
RT23a		L/N (as RT22) (S, T, U and W)				
		L/N	£30	£60	£95	£190
	(noted 1999)	U/-	Fine+	£40	- - - -	- - - -
	(noted 2001)	W/4-	- - -	"E.F."	£120	- - - -
	(noted 1999)	W/66	- - -	- - -	"Unc	£195
	(noted 1998)	W/- -	- - -	- - -	"abt.Uncirc"	£165
	(noted 1999)	W/68	- - -	"gd.E.F."	£125	- - - -
	(noted 2000)	W/4-	- - -	"E.F."	£120	- - - -

RT23a

| RT23b | Watermark has misshaped shamrock (L/12,32,52,72, and 92) | - - - | £260 | - - - - |

RT23b This leaf does not have the typical "heart" shape

Back: common to all from RT16 to RT23b

H. M. TREASURY NOTES

(Emergency) ONE POUND 5" x 2½" • 127mm x 63mm
Watermark: Royal Cypher - POSTAGE
Small vignette at left - very large value at right
Black & white - one side only - on stamp paper

No.	Date		Fine	V.F.	E.F.	About Uncirc.
	1914 (Aug) **John Bradbury:**					
RT25a.	Capital A.	(with stop)	£250	£600	£1250	- - - -
	(noted 1998) "Fine, repaired"		£130	- - - -	- - - -	- - - -
RT25b.	Capital B.	(with stop)	£225	£500	£1250	- - - -
RT25c.	Capital C.	(with stop)	£350	£750	£1500	- - - -
	(noted 2001)	C.737704	"gd.V.F."	£1250	- - - -	- - - -
RT26a	Capital A	(no stop)	£225	£500	£1250	- - - -
RT26b	Capital B	(no stop)	£250	£500	£1250	- - - -
RT26c	Capital C	(no stop)	£250	£500	£1250	- - - -
RT27a	L/N Nº	four digits	- - - -	£650		- - - -
	(noted 1999)	O/21	"gd.V.F." £320	- - - -		- - - -
RT27b	L/N Nº	five digits	£250	£700	£1,250	
	(noted 1998)		"E.F., edge tear"	£450	- - - -	
	(noted 1999)		- - -	- - - "superb abt.Unc"	£925	
RT27c	L/N Nº	six digits	£200	£450	£950	
	(sundry 1999)		"gd.VF" £275	£450	- - - -	

(Christie's 1987 "with romantic connections") A/15 Nº 000001 E.F. £1,300
Similar to RT27c · A Trial W/87 000000 at auction 1994 £1980
(West 1998) "Star Trial" · colour trial · w/mk stars/circles £1.100

RT27d	L/N Nº	seven digits	£500	- - - -	- - - -
RT28a	L/N Nº	four digits	£1750	- - - -	- - - -
	(Spink 96) L/30 "professionally repaired"		£1500	"VF"	- - - -
RT28b	L/N Nº	five digits	£600	£950	- - - -

RT25b.

H. M. TREASURY NOTES

(Emergency) ONE POUND 5" x 2½" • 127mm x 63mm
Details as page 12

No.	Date		Fine	V.F.	E.F.	About Uncirc.
RT29a	L/N Nº 6 small digits			£600	£950	- - - -
	(noted 1999)	"Fine" £295		- - - -	- - - -	- - - -
RT29b	L/N Nº 7 small digits			£750	£1200	- - - -
RT30	LL/N Nº six digits			£500	£700	- - - -
	(Notability 96) BB/10 "Fine" £160			- - - -	- - - -	- - - -
RT31	LL/N No. four digits (the stop *follows* the 'o' in RT31)					
		"guesstimate" £2,500		- - - -	- - - -	

SECOND ISSUE — ONE POUND

5⅞" x 3¼" • 149mm x 85mm
Watermark: wavy lines - Royal Cypher - ONE POUND - four emblems
Black & white - one side only - banknote paper
UNITED KINGDOM OF GREAT BRITAIN AND IRELAND

1914 (Oct) **John Bradbury:**

(Spink 1998) Trial sheet, undated, black & white two notes
"small tear" · hammer price £1,100

RT32   L/N   plus five digits (A, with gaps, to Z)

		- - -	£100	£200	£350
(noted 2000)	D/55	- - -	"E.F."	£280	- - - -
(noted 1999)	M/41	- - -	"E.F."	£280	- - - -
(noted 1999)	Z/39	"V.F."	£80	- - - -	- - - -

RT33 L1/N plus five digits (A1, with gaps, to L1)

			£120	£200	£350
(noted 1998)		£60	£125	£275	- - - -
(noted 1999)	C1/- -	£60	- - - -	- - - -	- - - -
(noted 2000)	Three consecutive slightly discoloured				£750

RT32
L/N plus five digits

13

H. M. TREASURY NOTES

DARDANELLES CAMPAIGN OVERPRINT ONE POUND

RT34 — Red overprint on RT32

No.	Date	Signature	Fine	V.F.	E.F.	About Unc.
				£2000	£4500	- - - -
	(Spink 1992)		- - - -	- - - -	- - - -	£6,160
	(Narbeth 1996)	J53	"F/VF"	£1995	- - - -	- - - -
	(Goulborn 2001)		£750	"repaired Fine"	- - - -	- - - -
	(Spink 1999)		"abt.V.F."	£1250	- - - -	- - - -

The overprint reads:

Piastres silver 120

Piastres silver one hundred and twenty

Notes bearing prefixes other than F, J, M, or Y; might be *GENUINE* NOTES with *FRAUDULENT* overprint. expert advice should be sought.

ONE POUND

6" x 3 3/8" • 152mm x 85mm

Watermark: diagonal lines in alternate bands - ONE POUND - emblems etc.
Brown, purple, green, white or cream paper • St. George and Dragon at left

UNITED KINGDOM OF GREAT BRITAIN AND IRELAND

No.	Date	Signature	Fine	V.F.	E.F.	About Uncirc.
	1917 (Jan)	**John Bradbury:**				
RT35	L/N	(A, B to H, Z)				
		A/-	- - -	£40	£95	£150
	(noted 20001)	A/27	"gd.V.F."	£65	- - - -	- - - -
	(sundry 1999)		£20	£40	£85	£145
		B/- to H/-	£10	£30	£75	£100
	(sundry 1999)		£10	£30	£80	£125
		Z/-	£15	£35	£85	£125
	(noted 1998)	Z/25	£25	£50	- - -	- - - -

H. M. TREASURY NOTES
ONE POUND
6" x 3³/₈" • 152mm x 85mm
Watermark: diagonal lines in alternate bands - ONE POUND - emblems etc.
Brown, purple, green, white or cream paper • St.George and Dragon at left
UNITED KINGDOM OF GREAT BRITAIN AND IRELAND

No.	Date	Signature		Fine	V.F.	E.F.	About Uncirc.
RT36	1919 (Sep)	**N. F. Warren Fisher:** L/N					
		(K to Z minus Q and V)					
		K/-	---	£25	£60		£95
	(noted 1999)	L/- to Y/--	---	£20	£50		£75
			"mid Nr.V.F."	£27		"Unc."	£90
	Sundry 2001:	H/40	"gd.V.F."	£32	----		----
	" "	M/40	---		"gd.E.F."	£55	----
	" "	U99	"gd.V.F."	£32	---		---
		Z/-	---	£25	£70		£105
	" "	Z/5	---	£25		"E.F."	£75	----

RT36

RT36a		L/N	Has broader N⁰ and very bold, sharp dot			
	(noted 1999)	R/70		£30	---	---	----

N⁰ 442079 RT36 L/N

N⁰ 201049 RT36A L/N

16   H. M. TREASURY NOTES
ONE POUND

Details as page 15

No.	Date	Signature N. F. Warren Fisher:	Fine	V.F.	E.F.	About Uncirc.
RT37		L1/N № (A1 to R1, no I1 or Q1, Z)				
		A1 / -	---	£30	£60	£90
	(noted 1999)	A1 / -	"Fine+"	£20	---	---
		B1 / - to R1 / -		£16	£40	£65
	(noted 1999)	R1 / -	"Fine+"	£14	---	---
		Z1 / -	---	£25	£75	£100
	(noted 2001)	Z1 / -	---	£75	---	----
	(noted 2001)	Z1 / 58	£22	"very good"	---	----
RT38		L1/N № (square dot)				
			---	£60	£95	£150
	(noted 1998)	H1	"V.F."	£55	---	----

(This may be nothing more than a slurred dot which would justify claims that "it doesn't exist")

L1/N RT37

Back: common to all from RT35 to RT40

Look out for and report finding ANCHOR just here

H. M. TREASURY NOTES   17
ONE POUND
6" x 3³/₈" • 152mm x 85mm
Brown, green, white • St.George and Dragon at left
Now reads 'UNITED KINGDOM OF GREAT BRITAIN
AND NORTHERN IRELAND'

No.	Date	Signature	Fine	V.F.	E.F.	Abt. Uncirc.
	1919 (Sep)	**N.F. Warren Fisher:**				
RT39	L1/N N°•	(S1, T1, U1, W1, X1, Z1)				
		S1/-	£20	£45	£75	£125
	(noted 2000)	S1/7	---	"gd.V.F."	£70	----
		T1/- to X1/-	£15	£40	£60	£90
	(noted 1998)	U1/99	"nr.Fine" £15	---	---	----
	(noted 2000)	X1/18	---	---	"E.F." £75	----
		Z1/-	£20	£45	£75	£125
	(noted 1999)	Z1/99	---	"gd.E.F."	£85	----
RT40	L1/N N°⁼	S1/-	£25	£50	£80	£125
	(noted 1999)	S1/52	"V.F."	£45	---	----
	(noted 1998)	T1/-	"V.F."	£55	---	----
	(noted 2000)	Z1/-	---	---	"Unc."	£200

Serials as RT39   (see note after RT38)

RT39 L1/N Dot

RT40 L1/N Dash

SECTION TWO
BANK OF ENGLAND NOTES

There were notes even before the Bank of England came into existence in 1694. Gentlemens' agreements in writing were promises (promissory notes) to re-imburse whoever eventually presented the notes:

"Thus a note from A to B promising to pay £20 for some ship(ment) would be used by B to pay C for corn. Then A would pay C instead (of B) the original amount of money".
(From D.M. Miller's "Bank of England and Treasury Notes 1694 - 1970").

D.M. Miller also tells how notes for despatch to London were first cut in half and the two halves sent by separate stage coaches to defeat the highwayman. Provided both consignments survived the coach trip, the notes were re-joined, encashed, and cancelled; the cancellation was re-inforced by punching or cutting a hole to prevent re-presentation.

The Bank was particularly upset by attempts to forge its notes. Simply being "caught in possession" meant certain transportation. This was harsh when one considers that some forgers were skilled enough to fool bank cashiers. There were so many prosecutions, however, that jurors ignored even the most damning evidence because the punishment was considered too severe. The Bank, itself, later endeavoured to ease the situation by arranging for the convict's family to accompany him, and by ensuring that they had some cash.

Knowingly possessing a forged note is still an offence. Sending a note to the bank for verification ("Is this an Operation Bernhard note?") will result in the issue of a *Memorandum of Detention* if the note proves to be counterfeit; then it will be destroyed. The Bank might well consider that forgeries of notes that are no longer legal tender offer no threat, but in the case of the Nazi forgeries it cannot be expected to forgive that massive affront to itself or the considerable damage intended against the whole British economy.

By 1725 there were notes in the range £20, £30, etc., to £100, £200, £300, £400, £500 and £1,000. Notes for £10, £15 and £25 were issued between 1759 and 1765, but none for under £10. Provincial banks and, even, tradesmen started issuing notes for any sum: in the extreme for one penny! Notes under £5 were eventually prohibited (except in Scotland), but it was too late. Notes issued without sufficient backing assets leads to bankruptcy. Over 100 banks met this fate, and a further 300 eventually closed.

BANK OF ENGLAND NOTES

Prosperity brought about by the efforts to pursue the wars with France caused a massive revival of little banks until their number exceeded 700. When war with France was drawing to a close, all the "steam" went out of the economy and customers found they needed the substance (gold) rather than the promise (notes). Hundreds of banks collapsed and brought even the Bank of England "to its knees".

It was found that many would have survived if they could have called-up their cash reserves in time. To remove that difficulty, the Bank of England opened branches to shorten the lines of communication iBirmingham, Bristol, Exeter, Gloucester, Leeds, Liverpool and Manchester branches were followed by others at Belfast, Cardiff, Hull, Leicester, Newcastle, Norwich, Portsmouth, Southampton and Swansea. The Exeter branch closed after transferring its business to Plymouth.

1. **RUNNING CASH NOTES;** receipts for deposits encashable for gold or silver.

2. **SEALED BILLS:** promissory notes issued against assets or deposits.

3. **ACCOMPTABLE NOTES:** certificates of deposits not intended as banknotes.

These three were written by hand. Amounts could be any sum whatsoever. On a £20 note the owner could draw £10, have this written in, and retain the note.

CHIEF CASHIERS; 1694 to 1777

John Kendrick 1694
John Kendrick with Thomas Speed 1694 to 1699
Thomas Madockes 1699 to 1739
James Collier with Daniel Race 1739 to 1751
Daniel Race with Elias Simes 1751 to 1759
Daniel Race 1759 to 1775
Charles Jewson 1775 to 1777

THE BANK OF ENGLAND 1694 to 1928
ABRAHAM NEWLAND 1778 TO 1807:

Ref	Value	Dates	Notes	Details
REB1	£1	1797		handwritten signature £57,500
		(noted 1993)	Note No.2 at auction	
REB2	£1	1798 - 1801	smaller plate	printed signature
REB2	(Spinks 1998)	"backed on paper v.gd"		hammer price £460
REB3	£1	1801 - 1803	new watermark	standard size
REB4	£1	1803 - 1807		value in watermark
REB5	£2	1797		handwritten signature
REB6	£2	1798 - 1801	smaller plate	printed signature
		(noted 1994)	1798 counter signed C.A. Phillips £17,050	
REB7	£2	1801 - 1803		standard size
REB8	£2	1803 - 1805		value in watermark
		(noted 1999)	"forgery good/fine" £325	----
REB9	£2	1805 - 1807		new/different design
REB10	£5	1793	----	---- ----
REB11	£10	1798 - 1801	smaller plate	printed signature
REB12	£10	1805 - 1807		Bank of England heading
REB13	£15		----	---- ----
	£100	(Spink 2000)	"abt.V.F."	estimate £16,000 - £22,000

HENRY HASE 1807 to 1829:

Ref	Value	Notes	Details
REB31	£1		handwritten date, countersigned
REB32	£1		handwritten date, not countersigned
REB33	£1		printed date and serials
		(noted 1998) London	"Fine" £500 ----
		(noted 1998) "V.gd." £200	---- ---- ----
		(noted 1998) "gd.Fine"	£550 ---- ----
REB34	£1	dated 1821	issued 1825/26
REB35	£2		handwritten date, countersigned
REB36	£2		handwritten date, not countersigned
REB37	£2		printed date and serials
REB38	£5		handwritten
REB39	£5		printed date and serials
REB40	£10	REB44 £30	REB48 £200
REB41	£15	REB45 £40	REB49 £300
REB42	£20	REB46 £50	REB50 £500
REB43	£25	REB47 £100	REB51 £1000
	£5 (Spink 2000) "Trial Hase printed in France £1,000 - £1,200		

THOMAS RIPPON 1829 TO 1835:

REB61	£5	REB65	£40	REB69	£300
REB62	£10	REB66	£50	REB70	£500
REB63	£20	REB67	£100	REB71	£1000
REB64	£30	REB68	£200		

THE BANK OF ENGLAND 1694 to 1928

MATTHEW MARSHALL 1835 to 1864:

REB91	£5	handwritten signature	REB98	£30
	(noted 1999) "forgery gd.Fine" £195	REB99	£40
REB92	£5	signature is printed	REB100	£50
REB93	£5	signature in watermark	REB101	£100
REB94	£10	handwritten signature	REB102	£200
REB95	£10	signature is printed	REB103	£300
REB96	£10	signature in watermark	REB104	£500
REB97	£20	REB97 to REB105 may	REB105	£1000

exist in the three forms given for £5 and £10

WILLIAM MILLER 1864 to 1866:

None bears Miller's signature

Signatures: W. P. Gattie · T. Kent · C. T. Whitmel

REB111	£5	REB114	£50	REB117	£300
REB112	£10	REB115	£100	REB118	£500
REB113	£20	REB116	£200	REB119	£1000

GEORGE FORBES 1866 to 1873: Signature in watermark

REB121	£5	Signed by member of staff		
REB122	£5	Signed by G. Forbes	REB127	£100
REB123	£10	Signed by member of staff	REB128	£200
REB124	£10	Signed by G. Forbes	REB129	£300
REB125	£20		REB130	£500
REB126	£50		REB131	£1000

From 1870 the Cashier's signature was printed and his title appended.

FRANK MAY 1873 to 1893:

REB141	£5	REB144	£50	REB147	£300

REB141 (noted 1999) cross cancelled forgery "E/31 V.F." £390

REB142	£10	REB145	£100	REB148	£500
REB143	£20	REB146	£200	REB149	£1000

REB146 (Spinks '98) "Specimen gd.EF" £14,000
REB149 (Spinks '98) "Specimen gd.EF" £18,500

HORACE GEORGE BOWEN 1893 to 1902:

REB151	£5	REB154	£50	REB157	£500
REB152	£10	REB155	£100	REB158	£1000
REB153	£20	REB156	£200		

From the list of cashiers on this page, only Hase appears with any frequency, perhaps every three months or so. Because of their rarity there is insufficient trading from which to compile any useful average. Only actual offers can provide a true guide to value.

22 THE BANK OF ENGLAND 1694 to 1928

No.	Date	Signature	Fine	V.F.	E.F.	E.F.+ Abt.Unc

JOHN GORDON NAIRNE 1902 to 1918:

REB160 An undated, $\overset{A}{1}$000000 One Pound - Nairne: promised Standard Gold Coin of the United Kingdom in exchange, and so ensured that Treasury notes were preferred by the Government, because it/they promised no such thing! (noted 1998) "E.F." £3,000

REB161	1909	£5	(noted 1998)	"abt V.F." £300	---	---
	1915	£5	(noted 1998)	---	"abt.EF"	£350	---
	1915	£5	(noted 2001)	"gd.Fine" £170	---	---

REB162	1917	£10		---	£225	£450	---
		£10	(noted 1998)	---	£215	---	---
		£10	(noted 2001)	"V.F."	£360	---	---

| REB163 | | £20 | | £200 | £400 | £950 | --- |
| REB164 | | £50 | | £250 | £500 | £1250 | --- |

Only 28 *provincial* notes of £50 are known:
(noted 1998) £800 £1500 ---

REB165		£100		---	£950	£1600	---
		Manchester (noted 1998)	---	"abt.EF"	£1200	
		Manchester (noted 1999)	"V.F."	£1150	---	---

REB166		£200		---	---	£2500	---
REB167		£500		---	---	£7500	---
REB168	1911	£1000 (Brooks '94)	Manchester		£12,000	---

REB161

THE BANK OF ENGLAND 1694 to 1928   23

No.	Date	Signature	Fine	V.F.	E.F.	About Uncirc.

ERNEST MUSGRAVE HARVEY 1918 to 1925:
FIVE POUNDS

No.	Date	Signature	Fine	V.F.	E.F.	About Uncirc.
REB170 TRIAL NOTE $^A_1$ 000000			Signed Harvey · paper bears Mahon w/mk			
(noted 1999)				"most attractive"		£16,100
REB171		London 1918	£25	£65	£125	- - - -
(noted 1998)		London	- - -	"nr.EF"	£89	- - - -
(noted 2000)		London	"V.F."	£60	- - -	- - - -
		Hull 1919	"V.F."	£495	- - -	- - - -
(noted 2001)		Hull 1919	"gd.Fine"	£430	- - -	- - - -
(noted 2001)		Hull U/96	£120	"Very good"	- - -	- - - -
		Leeds 1918	£40	£80	£160	£250
		Leeds 1919	£50	£100	£200	£300
(West 1999)		Leeds 1919		"V.F."	£150	- - - -
(noted 1999)		Manchester 1920	"V.F."	£180		- - - -
(noted 2000)		Manchester	- - -	"abt.EF"	£400	- - - -
(noted 2000)		Manchester U/19	£135	"Fine"	- - -	- - - -
(Narbeth '98)		Newcastle 1919		£350	- - -	- - - -
(West 2000)		Newcastle	"V.F."	£550	- - -	- - - -
(Brooks '94)		Plymouth 1925		- - -	"Unc"	£1,450

24 THE BANK OF ENGLAND · 1694 TO 1928

No.	Signature				Fine	V.F.	E.F.
	Ernest Musgrave Harvey						
REB172	£10	1919	London		£50	£115	£200
	£10	1921	London		----	----	£200
	£10	1922	London		"gd.VF"	£195	----
	£10	1924	London		----	----	£275
	£10	1925	London		----	----	£250
REB173	£20				£100	£250	£600
REB174	£50				£160	£350	£750
REB175	£100				£200	£500	£1250
(noted 2001)	£100				----	"E.F."	£800
REB176	£200					£550	£750
(noted 1999)	£200				"gd.VF"	£750	----
REB177	£500				£1500	£5000	----
REB178	£1000				----	----	----

REB172

Early Bank of England notes are found to have one cut, straight, edge and three untrimmed, or 'torn' ones. The practice of printing in pairs means that half of them will have a left-handed cut edge, whilst the other half will have their cut edge at the right.

SECTION THREE 25
BANK OF ENGLAND NOTES from 1928

The Bank of England's book "Promises To Pay" shows that there was a serious intention to replace 'valuable' silver currency with notes to the value of ONE SHILLING, TWO SHILLINGS and FIVE SHILLINGS. The designs were to be identical front and back, without watermark and not numbered. A thread was, however, to be incorporated.

The ONE SHILLING and TWO SHILLING notes were not taken beyond the proof stage. Notes for TWO SHILLINGS AND SIXPENCE (2/6 - HALF CROWN) and for FIVE SHILLINGS were produced in millions and distributed to a number of branches of various banks "just in case".

None was issued. All were recalled to be pulped. Some escaped to become "Collectors' Dreams".

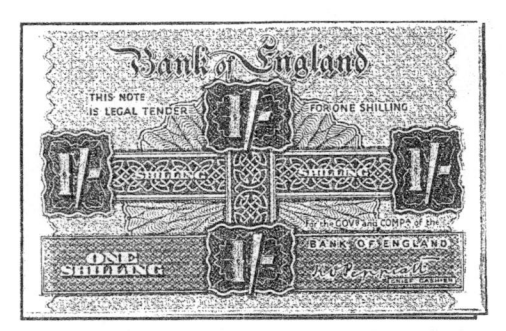

The recalled ONE SHILLING note

The recalled TWO SHILLING note

BANK OF ENGLAND NOTES

| No. | Date | Signature | V.F. | E.F. | Uncirc. |

HALF CROWN (Two Shillings and Sixpence)

Black on pale blue • 4½" x 2⅞" • 114mm x 73mm
Four 2/6 symbols • design the same on both sides

1941 K. O. Peppiatt:
RB1 No serial numbers   £2,000   £4,250   - - - -

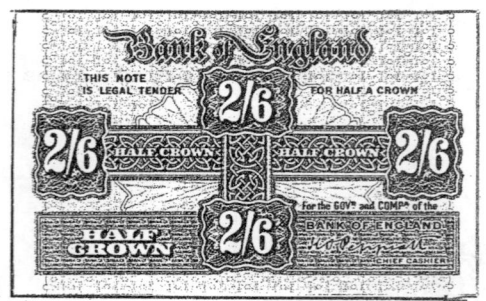

RB1

FIVE SHILLINGS

Olive-green on pale pink • 4½" x 2⅞" • 114mm x 73mm
Large central 5 • Design the same on both sides

1941 K. O. Peppiatt:
RB2 No serial numbers   £2,000   £4,250   - - - -

RB2

BANK OF ENGLAND NOTES — 27
SERIES 'A'   TEN SHILLINGS • "Britannia"
Red-brown • $5^{1}/_{2}$" x $3^{1}/_{16}$" • 138/140mm x 78mm

No.	Date	Signature	Fine	V.F.	E.F.	Abt. Uncirc.
	1928 (Nov)	**C. P. Mahon:**				
RB3	LNN	(A01 to Z99 · Y(?) to V13)				
	(noted 1996)	A00 000000 SPECIMEN	"gd.VF"	£950	"o/p once"	
		A01	£200	£375	£500	- - - -
	(noted 2000)	A01	- - - -	- - - -	"abt.Unc."	£700
		Z01	£10	£45	£150	£200
		Z - -		£35	£110	£195
	(West 1998)	Z90	- - - -	("superb unc.")	£220
		Y - -; X - -;	£30	£50	£80	£120
		W - -;	£35	£60	£90	£140
	(noted 1999)	W98	- - - -	- - - -	"Unc."	£145
		V - -		£220	£600	- - - -
	(noted 2000)	V02	- - - -	"nr.E.F."	£875	- - - -
		V13		£350	£750	- - - -
	1930 (July)	**B. G. Catterns:**				
		(V14 to K99)				
RB5	LNN	V14	£30	£60	£90	£150
		V - -		£35	£75	£95
		U - - to L - -		£15	£40	£55
		K - - (last K99)		£20	£60	£90

RB5 LNN

Back : common to all from RB3 to RB20

BANK OF ENGLAND NOTES
SERIES 'A' — TEN SHILLINGS • "Britannia"
Red-brown • 5½" x 3¹/₁₆" • 138/140mm x 78mm

No.	Date	Signature	Fine	V.F.	E.F.	Abt. Uncirc.
	1934 (Oct)	**K. O. Peppiatt:** (J01 to A99)				
	(Narbeth 1998)	Q00 000 000	Specimen		"abt. Unc"	£1,150
RB7	LNN	J--		£25	£50	£75
	(noted 1998)	J90	----	"E.F."	£75	----
		H-- to B--		£20	£50	£80
	(noted 1998)	C70	"V.F."	£18	---	
	(noted 2000)	B99	----	"E.F."	£45	----
		A--	----	£25	£50	£75
	(noted 1998)	A97	"gd.VF"	£35	---	---
RB8	NNL	(01Z to 99O)				
		--Z	----	£25	£65	£90
	(noted 1999)	99Z	----	"gd.V.F."	£40	----
		--Y to --R	----	£20	£50	£80
	(noted 1998)	83R	----	---	£60	----
	(noted 2000)	37O	----	"E.F."	£45	----
	(noted 1998)	02O	----	---	---	£60

See page 92 for plate/design size differences for numbers RB7 and RB8.

RB8 NNL

	1940 (Apr.)	**K. O. Peppiatt:**	MAUVE (with metal thread)			
RB10	LNNL	(Z01D to A86D) · Z01E to X21E)				
		Z01D		£25	£50	£75
		Z--D		£15	£30	£50
		Y--D to B--D		£10	£20	£30
		A--D		£14	£25	£40
	(noted 1999)	no serial number		"E.F."	£225	---
		Z--E, Y--E		£12	£25	£35
		X--E		£35	£80	£125
	(noted 1995)	X21E		£45	£100	£150

BANK OF ENGLAND NOTES 29

SERIES 'A' TEN SHILLINGS • "Britannia"
Red-brown • 5½" x 3¹/₁₆" • 138/140mm x 78mm • (no thread)

No.	Date	Signature	V.F.	E.F.	Uncirc.
	1948 (June)	**K. O. Peppiatt:**	RED-BROWN (no thread)		
RB12	NNL	(05L to 71L)			
		--L	---	£60	£95
	(Narbeth 96)	71L 114271	£125	"gd.VF"	---
	(noted 2000)	60L	"E.F."	£85	----
	1948 (Oct)	**K. O. Peppiatt:**	RED-BROWN (with thread)		
RB14	NNL	(71L to 91E) compare with RB12			
		--L	£75	£125	£200
		--K,--J,--H	£10	£20	£40
		--E	£20	£40	£80
	See page 92 for plate/design differences to RB14				
RB15	Replacement	(01A to 03A)	£200	£500	£750

RB14 NNL Plate 2

RB14 NNL Plate 3

	1950 (Mar.)	**P. S. Beale:**		RED-BROWN	
RB16	NNL	(92E to 99B)			
		92E	£70	£150	£250
		--D,--C,--B	£5	£12	£25
RB17	LNNL	(Z01Z to D85Z)		RED-BROWN	
		Z01Z	£40	£85	£150
		Z--Z	£12	£35	£50
		Y--Z to E--Z	£5	£18	£24
	(noted 1999)	JZ 000011	£15	---	---
RB18	Replacement	(04A to 35A)			
		04A	£200	£350	£450
		--A	£40	£75	£125

30 BANK OF ENGLAND NOTES

$5^{1}/_{2}"$ x $3^{1}/_{16}"$

SERIES 'A' "Britannia" TEN SHILLINGS

138/140mm x 78mm

No.	Date	Signature	V.F.	E.F.	Uncirc.
	1955 (Nov)	**L. K. O'Brien:**			
RB19	LNNL	(D86 to A96Z · Z01Y to A99Y · Z01X to Y25X)			
		D86Z	£30	£70	£125
		D - - Z	£20	£45	£65
		C - - Z, B - - Z	£6	£10	£16
		A - - Z	£8	£12	£25
		A96Z	- - -	£15	£35
		Z - - Y	£7	£20	£30
(noted 2001)		Y - - Y to B - - Y	£5	£10	£18
		N - - Y "miscut"	"E.F." £145		- - - -
		A - - Y	£6	£12	£18
		Z - - X	£9	£15	£25
		Y - - X	£10	£25	£40
RB20	NNL replacement (36A to 68A)				
		36A	- - -	£100	£150
		- - A	£30	£60	£95
		53A	"gdE.F."	£95	- - - -

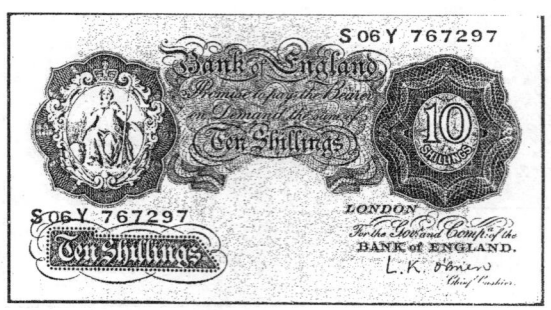

RB19 LNNL S06Y

RB20 NNL replacement 62A

BANK OF ENGLAND NOTES 31

SERIES 'C' TEN SHILLINGS: Portrait H.M. The Queen
Watermark : repetitive laureate head at left (viewed from front)
Red-brown • 5½" x 5⅝" • 140mm x 66mm

No.	Date	Signature	Fine	V.F.	E.F.	Uncirc.
	1961 (Oct)	**L. K. O'Brien:**				
RB21	LNN	(A01 to K64)				
	(noted 2001)	A00 000000 o/p SPECIMEN	---			£725
		A01	£5	£10	£20	£30
		A--	£3	£6	£9	£12
	(noted 1998)	A95	---	---	"Unc"	£12
		B-- to J--	---	£2	£4	£6
		K--	---	£5	£10	£15
	(noted 1998)	K63	---	---	"Unc"	£25
RB22	LNN	(M01 to M18)	Replacement note			
		M01	---	£20	£50	£75
	(noted 1998)	M03	---	"E.F."	£25	---

RB21 LNN

Back: common to all from RB21 to RB28

	1963 (Apr)	**J. Q. Hollom:**				
RB23	LNN	(K65 to Z99)				
		K65	---	£20	£50	£80
	(noted 1998)	K66, K72, K74 each	---	£10	£30	
		L-- to Y--	---	---	£3	£6
		Z--	---	---	£5	£10
	(noted 1998)	Z98	---	---	£10	£20
	(West 1996)	K-- to Z-- "11 note prefix set, abt. Unc." £35				

BANK OF ENGLAND NOTES

SERIES 'C'   **TEN SHILLINGS: Portrait H.M. The Queen**
Watermark : repetitive laureate head at left (viewed from front)
Red-brown • 5½" x 2⅝" • 140mm x 66mm

No.	Date	Signature	Fine	V.F.	E.F.	Uncirc.
	1963 (Apr)	**J. Q. Hollom:**				
RB24	NNL	(01A to 26R)				
		01A	---	£10	£30	£50
		--A	---	£2	£5	£10
		--B to --N	---	---	£2	£4
	(noted 1998)	10R	---	---	"Unc"	£30
	(noted 1998)	19R	---	"E.F."	£15	---
	(noted 2001)	24R	---	"E.F."	£22	---
		--A to --R prefix set	---	---	---	£50
RB25	LNN	(M19 to M55)		Replacement note		
		M--	---	£10	£20	£30
	(noted 2000)	M26	---	"gd.E.F."	£25	---
	(noted 1998)	M47	---	"gd.E.F."	£22	---
	(noted 1999)	M53	---	---	"abt.Unc."	£40

RB24 NNL

RB25 replacement note M--

BANK OF ENGLAND NOTES 33

SERIES 'C'   **TEN SHILLINGS: Portrait H.M. The Queen**

No.	Date	Signature	Fine	V.F.	E.F.	Uncirc.
	1967 (Feb)	**J. S. Fforde:**				
RB26	NNL	(26R to 99Z)				
		26R	£10	£30	£60	£85
		--R	---	---	£9	£20
	(noted 1999)	89R	---	"nr.E.F."	£3	---
	(noted 2000)	99R	---	---	---	£15
		'mid'	---	---	£3	£5
	(noted 2001)	01X	---	---	"Unc"	£8
		--Z	---	---	£4	£10
RB27	LNNL	(A01N to D38N)				
	(noted 2001)	A01N	---	"E.F."	£75	---
		A--N	---	£2	£3	£6
		B--N, C--N	---	---	---	£4
	(noted 1999)	B74N 000097	---	---	"abt.Unc"	£6
	★	C01N	offered variously at		£6/£8/£12/£15	
	(noted 2001)	D01N	---	---	"Unc"	£8
		D--N	---	---	£3	£6
		D38N	high/low serial		---	£30/£25
RB28	LNN	(M56 to M80)	Replacement note			
		M56	£3	£30	£50	£95
		M--	---	---	£10	£15
	(noted 2001)	M80	---	---	---	£18

★ RB21 to RB27 sport such combinations as: H2O, CO2, OIL, IOW, COIN, BOIL, COIL, LOIN; and 1OB (Tenby).

RB27 LNNL C01N

RB28 LNN replacement note

34
SERIES 'A'
BANK OF ENGLAND NOTES
ONE POUND • "Britannia"
Green • $5\frac{15}{16}$" x $3\frac{5}{16}$" • 151mm x 85mm

No.	Date	Signature	Fine	V.F.	E.F.	About Uncirc.
	1928 (Nov)	**C. P. Mahon:**				
RB31	LNN	(A01 to H32)				
	(noted 1999)	A00 000000	---	---		£2,200
		A01		£400	£650	£1,300
	(noted 2000)	A01	---	"E.F."	£600	----
		A- -	£22	£35	£70	£110
	(noted 1998)	A02		£40	£75	----
		B- - to G- -		£22	£50	£75
	(noted 2000)	D40	---	---	"abtUnc."	£80
	(noted 1998)	E98	---	---	"Unc."	£145

---
100 pairs of £1 and 10/- notes having matching serial numbers presented in parchment envelopes inscribed:
'BANK OF ENGLAND 22 November 1928'
All are A01   guesstimate   £2,500   £3,000

	1930 (July)	**B. G. Catterns:**				
RB33	LNN	(H33 to Z99)				
		H33	£10	£25	£60	£95
		H- -	£8	£20	£50	£75
	(noted 1998)	T33	---	"E.F."	£30	----
	(noted 2001)	Z94	---	"E.F."	£40	----
RB34	NNL	(01A to 99A)				
		01A	£20	£45	£95	£150
		- -A	£10	£40	£75	£100
	(noted 2000)	50A	---	"E.F."	£120	----

RB33 LNN

BANK OF ENGLAND NOTES 35
SERIES 'A' ONE POUND • "Britannia" Details as page 34

No.	Date	Signature	Fine	V.F.	E.F.	About Uncirc.
★	GUERNSEY OVERPRINTS	September 18th, 1941				
RB31a	**MAHON**	A-- to H--	(48 only) £350		£500	----
	(noted 1999)	D52	---	"abt.E.F."	£450	----
RB33a	**CATTERNS**	H-- to Z--	(69 only) £325		£475	----
	(noted 1999)	J25	"gd.V.F."	£350	----	----
RB34a		--A	(5 only)	----	----	----
RB36a	**PEPPIATT**	--B to --Z	(330)	£150	£300	----
RB37a		A--A to L--A	(1,885)	£125	£250	£350
	(Spink 1996)	unspecified	---	----	"Unc."	£400
RB37b		E03A only	(75 only) £300		£525	----
RB37c		E15A only	£125	£250	£325	£425
★	a = date has stop on front only				1941.	1941.
	b = date has stop on both front and back				1941.	1941.
	c = date has stop on back only				1941	1941.
	1934 (Oct)	**K. O. Peppiatt:**				
RB36	NNL	(01B TO 99Z)				
		01B	£10	£25	£50	£75
	(noted 1998)	36B	---	"E.F."	£55	---
		--C to --Y	---	£10	£20	£30
	(noted 2001)	98T 999996	---	---	"Unc."	£55
		--Z	---	£20	£45	£70
RB37	LNNL	(A03A to L39A)				
		A03A	---	£20	£45	£65
		A--A	---	£10	£20	£30
		B--A to K--A		£9	£18	£25
		L--A	---	£15	£30	£50
	(noted 2001)	L39A	"V.F."	£32	---	---

RB36 NNL

BANK OF ENGLAND NOTES

SERIES 'A'   "Britannia" ONE POUND
BLUE • $5\frac{15}{16}$" x $3\frac{5}{16}$" • 151mm x 85mm   (with METAL THREAD)

No.	Date	Signature	Fine	V.F.	E.F.	Uncirc.
	1940 (March) K. O. Peppiatt :					
RB41	LNNL	(A01D · A01E · A01H)				
	(noted 2001)	A00D 000000	SPECIMEN		"Unc"	£1,250
		A01D	£5	£15	£30	£45
		A- -D	£3	£10	£20	£35
		A01E	£4	£12	£25	£40
		A- -E, A- -H	£3	£9	£18	£30
		A01H	£4	£12	£20	£35
	(noted 2001)	A99D	- -	"E.F."	£65	- - -
	(noted 1999)	A99H	"abt.V.F."	£20	- - -	- - -
	(noted 2000)	O99H	- -	"E.F."	£12	- - -
	(noted 2000)	X01H	"V.F."	£20	- - -	- - -

GUERNSEY OVERPRINT

RB41a		A- -D	(35 only)		£325	£550	- - - -
RB42a		C- -D	(85 only)		£250	£450	- - - -
	(noted 1999)	C63D	- -		"gd.E.F."	£490	- - - -

RB41 LNNL

RB37b

BANK OF ENGLAND NOTES

SERIES 'A' "Britannia" ONE POUND
BLUE • $5\frac{15}{16}$" x $3\frac{5}{16}$" • 151mm x 85mm (with METAL THREAD)

No.	Date		Fine	V.F.	E.F.	Uncirc.
	1940 (Sept.)	(by offset-photolithography)				
RB42	LNNL	(B01D to Z87D · B01E to W38E · B01H to X94H)				
		B01D	£5	£10	£25	£50
		-01-s	£4	£8	£15	£30
		'mids'	£2	£4	£8	£12
(Narbeth '92)		"Extra paper, small fin, Fine £165"	- - -		- - - -	
(noted 1998)		Z51D	- - -	- - -	"Unc."	£35
		B01E	£5	£10	£25	£50
		-01-s	£4	£8	£15	£30
		'mids'	£2	£4	£9	£14
		B01H	£5	£10	£25	£50
		-01-s	£4	£8	£15	£30
		'mids'	£2	£4	£8	£12
(noted 1998)		X93H	- -	- - -	"Unc."	£45
K. O. Popeye · blue skit note for ONE PUNCH · "E.F." £20						- - -

SERIES 'A' "Britannia" ONE POUND (without metal thread)
GREEN • $5\frac{15}{16}$" x $3\frac{5}{16}$" • 151mm x 85mm

1948 (June) K. O. Peppiatt :

No.			Fine	V.F.	E.F.	Uncirc.
RB44	LNNL	(R01A to S48A)				
		R01A	£5	£15	£45	£65
(noted 2000)		R01A low serial	- -	- - -	"Unc."	£110
		R- -A	- -	£10	£20	£40
(noted 1998)		R87A	- -	"E.F.+"	£25	- - -
(noted 1999)		R99A	- -	"gd.E.F."	£70	- - -
(noted 1998)		S01A	- -	"E.F."	£85	- - -
		S- -A	- -	£20	£40	£60
(noted 1999)		S- -A	- -	"E.F."	£35	- - -
(noted 1999)		S70A	- -	"gd.E.F."	£20	- - -

Prefixes overlap those of RB46 (page 38) but the thread, or absence thereof, differentiates between these, otherwise identical, notes.

BANK OF ENGLAND NOTES
SERIES 'A' "Britannia" ONE POUND (with METAL THREAD)
GREEN • $5\frac{15}{16}$" x $3\frac{5}{16}$" • 151mm x 85mm

No.	Date	Signature	Fine	V.F.	E.F.	Uncirc.
★1948 (Sept) K. O. Peppiatt:						
RB46	LNNL	(S40A to Z 99A · A01B to H36B)				
		S40A	£10	£20	£60	£80
		S--A		£10	£30	£40
	(noted 1999)	S99A	---	---	£65	---
		T--A to Y--A		£4	£12	£18
		-01As	---	£5	£15	£20
		Z--A	£3	£6	£16	£22
	(noted 1999)	Z93A	---	---	"abt.Unc."	£28
	(noted 2000)	Missing upper serial number	£85	---	---	---
		A01B	£8	£16	£35	£60
		A--B	---	£5	£10	£20
		B--B to E--B	---	£5	£10	£20
	(noted 1998)	H33B	---	---	"Unc."	£40
	(noted 1999)	H36B	"V.F."	£70	---	---

★ See page 92 regarding plate sizes etc.

Prefixes overlap those of RB44 (page 37) but the thread differentiates between these, otherwise identical, notes.

RB46 LNNL — Z83A 229842

RB47	LNNL (S01S to S09S)	Replacement note			
	(noted 2001)	S01S	"E.F." £300		----
	(noted 1998)	S02S	"gd.V.F." £98		----
	(noted 1999)	S02S	"V.F." £50	---	----
	(noted 1999)	S03S	---	"gd.E.F."	£200
	(noted 1998)	S05S	"abt.E.F." £120		----

BANK OF ENGLAND NOTES 39
SERIES 'A' "Britannia" ONE POUND (with METAL THREAD)
GREEN • $5\frac{15}{16}$" x $3\frac{5}{16}$" • 151mm x 85mm

No.	Date	Signature	Fine	V.F.	E.F.	Uncirc.
	1950 (Mar)	**P. S. Beale:**				
RB51	LNNL	(H37B to Z99B · A01C to Z99C · A01J to L63J)				
		H37B	£25	£60	£120	£175
		H- -B	- - -	£6	£12	£20
	(noted 1999)	H99B	- - -	- - -	"Unc."	£50
		-01-s	- - -	- - -	£10	£20
		J- -B to Y- -B	- - -	£3	£5	£7
	(noted 1998)	Z98B	- - -	"abt.E.F."	£30	- - -
		A01C	£4	£9	£20	£45
		A- -C		£4	£9	£18
	(West 1993)	A96C	- - -	- - -	"gd.E.F."	£20
		B- -C to Y- -C	- - -	£3	£5	£7
		-01-s	- - -	£5	£10	£20
		Z- -C	- - -	£4	£12	£22
		A01J	- - -	- - -	£10	£20
		A- -J	- - -	- - -	£5	£10
		B- -J to K- -J	£2	£4	£8	
		L- -J	- - -	£5	£12	£18
		L63J	£4	£9	£20	£40

RB51 LNNL

RB52	LNNL	(S10S to S70S) Replacement note			
	(noted 1998)	S10S	£100	£130	- - - -
	(noted 1998)	S24S	£30	- - -	- - - -
	(noted 1998)	S42S	- - -	£30	£60
	(noted 1998)	S44S	£20	- - -	£50
	(noted 2000)	S46S 311117/18	consec pair	"abt.Unc."	£90
	(noted 1998)	S68S	- - -	- - -	£75

BANK OF ENGLAND NOTES
SERIES 'A' "Britannia" ONE POUND (with METAL THREAD)
GREEN • 5$\frac{15}{16}$" x 3$\frac{5}{16}$" • 151mm x 85mm

No.	Date	Signature	V.F.	E.F.	Uncirc.
	1955 (Nov)	**L. K. O'Brien:**			
RB53	LNNL	(L64J to Z99J · A01K to Z99K · A01L to K13L)			
		L64J	£35	£80	£150
		L--J	£4	£12	£18
		-01-s	£6	£14	£20
		'mids'	£2	£4	£7
	(noted 1998)	Z99J	"V.F."	£40	- - - -
		A01K	£4	£12	£16
		A--K	£3	£9	£12
		-01-s	£2	£8	£10
		'mids'	- -	£3	£6
		Z--K	£3	£9	£12
		A01L	£25	£60	£95
	(Spink 1996)	A30L 000007	"abt.VF"	£30	- - - -
	(noted 1999)	A61L	"E.F."	£25	- - - -
		B--L to J--L	£2	£4	£7
	(noted 2000)	D--L "miscut"	"E.F."	£59	- - - -
		K--L	£10	£25	£50
		K13L	£20	£40	£80
RB54	LNNL	(S71S to S99S · S01T to S23T) Replacement			
		S71S	£50	£125	£175
	(noted 1998)	S73S	£15	- - -	£50
	(noted 1998)	S85S	- -	£45	£65
	(noted 2001)	S99S	"E.F."	£110	- - - -
		S01T	£50	£125	£175
	(noted 1998)	S07T	- -	£50	- - - -
	(noted 2000)	S16T	"E.F."	£45	- - - -

Back: design common to all from RB31 to RB54

BANK OF ENGLAND NOTES 41

SERIES 'C'   ONE POUND: Portrait H.M. The Queen

Green • $5\frac{15}{16}$" x $2\frac{13}{16}$" • 151mm x 73mm

No.	Date	Signature	V.F.	E.F.	Uncirc.
	1960 (Mar)	**L. K. O'Brien:**			
RB61	LNN	(A01 to Z99)			
	(West 1998)	A00 000000 "o/p SPECIMEN E.F."			£1,200
		A01 low serial	£50	£100	£160
		A--	£2	£10	£25
		-01s	--	£3	£6
		B-- to Y--	"mids"	£2	£4
	(Error 2001)	B-- small fin and miscut	£65	----	
	(Error 1992)	D-- missing serial nos.	£65	----	
		Z--	£2	£6	£10
	(noted 2000)	Z03	--	"abt.Unc."	£22
RB62	NNL	(01A to 99Z)			
		01A	£20	£50	£85
		--A	£2	£4	£8
		01-s	--	£3	£6
		--B to --Y	"mids"	£2	£4
		01L	--	--	£10
		--Z	"mids" £2	£4	£8
	Error (1992)	--Z "Large fin" £165	--	----	
RB63R	LNNL	with 'R' (research) at back (A01N, A05N, A06N only)			
		A01N	£50 £100	£200	£400
	(noted 2001)	A01N	--- "E.F."	£250	----
	(noted 1998)	A06N	--- £95	£150	---
RB64	LNNL	(B01N to B76N)			
		B01N	--	--	£50	£80
		B--N	--	--	£15	£30
RB65	LNN	(M01 to M68) Replacement note			
	(noted 1998)	M01	"gd.VF"	£45	----
	(noted 1999)	M64 high serial	--	"abt.Unc."	£30

RB65 replacement note

The bank of England requires that pictures of notes bearing the Queen's image be overprinted "SPECIMEN". The notes are not specimen notes unless so described in the text.

42 BANK OF ENGLAND NOTES
SERIES 'C' — ONE POUND: Portrait H.M. The Queen
Green • $5\frac{15}{16}$" x $2\frac{13}{16}$" • 151mm x 73mm

No.	Date	Signature	Fine	V.F.	E.F.	Uncirc.
	1963 (Feb)	**J. Q. Hollom:**				
RB66	LNNL	(B77N to B10Y with gaps)				
		B77N	£15	£40	£95	£145
		B- -N	- -	£20	£40	£60
		C- -N to L- -W	- -	£2	£4	£6
		A- -Y	- -	£3	£6	£9
		B- -Y	- -	£15	£30	£45
		B10Y	- -	£20	£40	£60
RB67	LNN	(M68 to M99) Replacement note				
		M- -	£5	£15	£30	£40
RB68	NNL	(01M to 99M) Replacement note				
	(noted 2001)	01M "Fine"	£15	- - -	- - -	- - -
	(noted 1998)	22M	- -	- - -	- - -	£20
RB69	LNNL	(M01R to M08R) Replacement note				
	(noted 1998)	M07R	- -	- - -	£35	£75
RB70G	LNNL with 'G' (Goebel machine) at back (A09N to L99X)					
		A09N	£5	£10	£25	£40
	The prefixes	A- -N	- -	£3	£6	£20
	missing from	D- -T, C- -W	- -	£2	£4	£6
	the RB66 series	L- -X	- -	£2	£5	£8
RB71G	LNNL	(M01N to M28N) Replacement note				
	(noted 1998)	M01N	- -	- - -	"Unc."	£75
	(noted 1999)	M01N	- -	"E.F."	£70	- - -
	(noted 1998)	M08N	- -	- - -	- - -	£25
	(noted 1998)	M28N	- -	- - -	- - -	£60

Back: common to all, with exception of 'G' on some, from RB61 to RB84.

'G' at back (Goebel machine)

BANK OF ENGLAND NOTES 43
SERIES 'C'   ONE POUND: Portrait H.M. The Queen
Green • 5$\frac{15}{16}$" x 2$\frac{13}{16}$" • 151mm x 73mm

No.	Date	Signature	V.F.	E.F.	Uncirc.
	1967 (Feb)	**J. S. Fforde:**			
RB72	LNNL	(B11Y to L--Y · A--Z to L99Z)			
		B11Y	£25	£75	£120
		B--Y	--	--	£30
	(noted 1999)	B22Y	--	"E.F.+"	£20
		C--Y to L--Y	--	£3	£5
	(noted 1999)	E99Y	--	--	£30
		-01-s	--	--	£9
		'mids'	--	£4	£6
		L--Z	£6	£10	£25
	(noted 1998)	L99Z	--	£20	£40
	(noted 2001)	missing prefix and serials	--	"Unc."	£180
RB73	LNNL	(M09R to M49R			
	(noted 1998)	M47R	--	--	£50
RB74G	LNNL with	'G' (Goebel machine) at back:			
		(E01Y to E99Y · K01Z ? to K99Z)			
	(noted 1998)	E01Y	"gd.V.F."	£10	---
		E--Y, K--Z	£2	£4	£7
	(noted 1998)	K99Z	"V.F." £20	--	---
RB75G	LNNL	(M29N to M42N) Replacement note			
	(noted 1998)	M29N	"abt.E.F."	£75	---
		M--N	£20	£40	£60
		M42N	---	"abt.Unc."	£125

RB72 LNNL

RB72 E99Y

BANK OF ENGLAND NOTES

SERIES 'C'   **ONE POUND: Portrait H.M. The Queen**

Green • $5\frac{15}{16}$" x $2\frac{13}{16}$" • 151mm x 73mm

No.	Signature		V.F.	E.F.	Uncirc.
	J. S. Fforde:				
RB76	LNNL reversal of control letter (type 2) (N01A to X42C)				
	N01A		£10	£30	£45
	N--A		£5	£15	£20
	N--B to X--B		--	£4	£6
(noted 1996)	N--J	"shark's fin"	--	£105	----
(noted 1999)	S93L		"E.F."	£9	----
(error 1993)	T38E	identical misnumbered pair			£175
	X42C		£15	£30	£60
(noted 1999)	X10C		"E.F."	£15	---
RB77	LNNL	(R01M to R53M · S01M to S72M · T01M to T04M and U01M only) Replacement notes			
	R--M		£5	£12	£20
	S--M		£3	£6	£10
(Spink 1996)	S51M 722997/722996 "RB77/RB82 pair"				£450
(noted 2000)	another FORD/PAGE consec pair "abtUnc."				£300
(sundry 1999)	T01M		£60	£125	£175
RB78G	LNNL with 'G' (Goebel machine) at back:				
	R--B		£2	£5	£9
(noted 2001)	R01L		---	"abt.Unc."	£80
(error 2001)	R31L	mismatched serials		£60	----
	R--L		--	£4	£8
(noted 1998)	R99L		"gd.E.F."	£28	---
(noted 1999)	U01E		--	"abt.Unc."	£100
(noted 1999)	U45E		"E.F."	£130	----
(error 1998)	misprinted consecutive pair			---	£200
(error 2001)	identically numbered pair			"Unc."	£300

RB76   LNNL reversal of control letter (type 2)

BANK OF ENGLAND NOTES 45

SERIES 'C' — ONE POUND: Portrait H.M. The Queen
Green • $5\frac{15}{16}$" x $2\frac{13}{16}$" • 151mm x 73mm

No.	Date		Fine	V.F.	E.F.	Uncirc.
RB79G	LNNL	(N01M to N14M · T29M to T32M) 'G' Replacement notes				
	(noted 1998)	N12M	---	---	"gd.V.F."	£15	----
	(noted 1998)	N06M	---	---	---	"gd.E.F."	£45
	(noted 1998)	N14M	---	---	"E.F."	£80	----
		T29M	---	---	---	£125	£175
		T--M	£25	£50	£100	£150
	(noted 1999)	T32M	---	---	---	£175	----

RB78G LNNL   shared number with mismatch

No.	Date	Signature	V.F.	E.F.	Uncirc. From/To
	1971	J. B. Page:			
RB81	LNNL	S--L	£45	£125	£175
		T--B to T--L	---	£2/3	£3/£5
	(Spink 1996)	"1 digit missing from lower serial"			£40
		U--A to W--H	---	£2/3	£3/£5
	(error 1993)	W66E/W77E on same note	----		£75
		X--A to X--L	---	£2/3	£3/£5
	(noted 2001)	X86A 666666	---	"Unc."	£85
		Y--A to Y--L	---	£2/3	£3/£5
	(Spink 1996)	Y41C 617295 "Pair, same prefix/serial"			£170
	(error 1993)	Y50D bears a broad green line			£50
		Z--A to Z--K	---	£2	£3/£5
	(error 1994)	pair share first number, 2nd different on each			£160
	(noted 2001)	Z--H 784487 "Radar"	---	"Unc."	£22
		Z--L		£2	£4	£7/£5

BANK OF ENGLAND NOTES

SERIES 'C' Details as page 45 **ONE POUND** : Portrait H.M. The Queen

No.	Date 1971	Signature J. B. PAGE:	V.F.	E.F.	Uncirc.
RB82	LNNL	(R44M to R99M · S32M to S98M · W01M to W84M X01M to X60M) Replacement notes			
	(noted 2001)	R56M and R60M	---	"Unc."	£40
		S--M Fine £3	£6	£10	£20
		W--M,	£3	£5	£15
	(noted 1998)	W01M	"gd.V.F."	£20	----
	(noted 2001)	X01M	---	£50	£75
		X--M	£3	£6	£15
	(noted 1998)	X18M	---	---	£15
	(noted 1999)	X60M	---	---	£60
RB83	LLNN	(AN01 to HZ62 but see ★ below)			
		AN01	---	£30	£50
		AN--	£2	£4	£6
	(noted 2000)	AN-- with blank reverse	"Unc."		£225
	(noted 1998)	AN94	---	---	£18
		AR-- to AZ--	---	£2	£5
		BN-- to BZ--	---	£2	£5
	(Spink 1996)	BS44 and BS45 100000 "Unc. each"			£175
	(Goulborn '96)	BS61/BS62 100000 "pair virt. unc."			£375
	(noted 1999)	paper reel joint	"abt.E.F."	£95	----
		CN-- to CZ--	---	£3	£5
	(noted 1999)	CN33 333333	"V.F."	£25	----
		DN-- to DZ--	---	£3	£5
	(error 1998)	DY15 mismatched numbers			£65
		EN-- to EZ--	---	£2	£3/£5
	(error 2000)	ES79 unusual 3 digit mismatch			£90
		HN-- to HY--	£2	£3	£4/£6
	(noted 1999)	HU-- 000001	--	"Unc."	£165
	(error 1998)	HT40 mismatched numbers			£80
		HZ62	---	---	£85
★	(noted 1999)	HZ63	"gd.V.F."	£185	----
RB84	LLNN	(MR01 to MR41 · MS01 to MS84 · MT01 to MT23 MU01 to MU18 · MW01 to MW19) Replacements			
	(noted 2000)	MS01	---	---	£90
	(noted 1998)	MS84	---	---	£60
	(noted 2000)	MT01	---	---	£90
	(noted 1996)	MT-- "same number three notes unc."			£195
	(noted 1998)	MU01	---	---	£20
	(noted 2000)	MW01	---	---	£60
		MW19	---	£35	£55

BANK OF ENGLAND NOTES
SERIES 'D' ONE POUND: Pictorial

No.	Date	Signature	Fine	V.F.	E.F.	Uncirc.

H. M. The Queen/Sir Isaac Newton
Mainly Green • 5¼" x 2⅝" • 133/135mm x 66/67mm

1978 (Feb)   **J. B. Page:**

RB85	LNN	(A01 to Z80)				
		A01	---	---	---	£10
	(noted 1993)	A01 Very low serial number (001205)				£60
	(noted 2000)	A06 000253	---	---	"abt.Unc."	£22
		A--	---	---	---	£4
		B-- to Y--		---	£2	£3
		'mid' -01s		---	£3	£6
	(error 1999)	four digits at right, last two at left				£140
	(noted 1998)	E44 444444		£16	"Fine"	---
	(noted 1999)	Z01	---	---	£9	£22
		Z--	---	£2	£4	£6
RB86	LNN	(M01 only) Replacement note				
	(noted 1998)	M01	---	---	"gd.E.F."	£190
	(noted 1999)	M01	---	---	"Unc."	£250
RB87	NNL	(01A to 80Y)				
	(noted 1998)	01A 001---		"nr.E.F."	£19	---
		31A 939997 with HAND-WRITTEN number exists				---
		--B to --X		---	£3	£4
		01L		---	---	£7
	(noted 1999)	10U (Several sources)			"Unc"	£10
	(noted 2001)	10W		---	"Unc"	£6
		--Y		---	£3	£4
	Experimental	(81E to 81Y)				
RB87E	1999 "sightings"	81E	---	---	---	£150
		81K	---	---	---	£150
		81Z	£50	£150		£250

RB85 LNN

SERIES 'D' ONE POUND: Pictorial

No.	Date	Signature	Fine	V.F.	E.F.	Uncirc.

H. M. The Queen/Sir Isaac Newton
Mainly Green • 5¼" x 2⅝" • 133/135mm x 66/67mm

RB88	LNNL	(A01N to E84N)				
	(Spink 1996)	A01N Low serial number			---	£45
		A01N	---	---	£15	£30
		B--N, C--N, D--N	---	£2	£3	£5
		C01N	---	£2	£6	£10
	(error 1998)	C08N	---		"shark's fin"	£120
	(noted 1998)	E01N	"V.F."	£7	---	---
		E84N	---	£4	£12	£20

RB88 LNN C01N

1981 (March) D. H. F. Somerset ('w' at back) :

RB89	LLNN	(AN01 to DY21)				
		AN01		---	£15	£25
	(noted 2000)	AN01 000481	---	---	---	£130
	(noted 1998)	AN01 001206		---	---	£65
	'mid'	--01s		---	---	£6
		AR-- to AZ--		---	£3	£5
		BN-- to BZ--		---	£3	£5
	(noted 2001)	BY18 ghosted image £75			minus letters	
		CN-- to CZ--		---	£2	£4
	(noted 2000)	CN13 "experimental aniline printing"				£180
	(Goulborn '99)	CS22 235689 *pencilled number* orange stripe				
	"	" "fine+" £33 (incredibly rare? - ed.)				
	(error 1998)	DS07 "gd.V.F." £90 "boat rudder"				
		DN-- to DX--		---	£3	£5
		DY01		---	---	£18
	(noted 1998)	DY21		---	"Unc"	£45
	(Bowen 1991)	DY21 7 consecutive				£250
	(noted 1993)	DY21 972925		---	---	£75
		"Dairy Crest" folder		---	---	£2

GLAND NOTES   49

SERIES 'D' ONE POUND: Pictorial

No.   Date   Signature   Fine   V.F.   E.F.   Uncirc.

H. M. The Queen/Sir Isaac Newton
Mainly Green • 5¼" x 2⅝" • 133/135mm x 66/67mm

RB90   LLNN   (MN04 to MN18)   Experimental
                     MN--   £400?   £800?   £1200?
         (auction 1999) MN17   "Fair"   £529 (hence the ? ?)

Paper pounds demonetized Midnight 11th March, 1988

From Derrick Byatt's "Promises to Pay" we learn that the last note printed was numbered DY21 999997, the next two being spoilt in production.

CS22 235689 numbered in pencil
The bold orange stripe is presumably used to indicate rejection.
A replacement note bearing the same number should exist !

Back: RB85 to RB90
Somerset notes have
a small 'w' and some
colour enhancements

A tiny 'w'

BANK OF ENGLAND NOTES

No.	Date	Signature	V.F.	E.F.	Abt. Uncirc.

FIVE POUNDS
Black and white • $8\frac{5}{16}$" x $5\frac{5}{16}$" • 212mm x 135mm
Serial number LARGE at upper left and upper right
Very small repeat of number at lower right

RB101	**1925 (Apr.) C. P. Mahon:**				
		1925 London	£70	£140	£220
	(noted 1998)	1925 London	"V.F.+"	£125	£225
	(West 1996)	1927 Hull	£300	"gdFine"	- - - -
	(noted 2001)	Leeds	"E.F."	£300	- - - -
	(noted 1998)	Liverpool	- - - -	£200	£300

RB101

RB102

BANK OF ENGLAND NOTES 51

No.	Date		Signature	V.F.	E.F.	Abt. Uncirc.
		FIVE POUNDS	Details as page 50			
RB102	**1929 (Mar) B. G. Catterns:**					
	(noted 1998)	13.5.30	London	"abt.E.F."	£195	- - - -
	(noted 1998)		London	"gdVF"	£105	- - - -
	(noted 1999)	1931	London	£85	"V.F."	- - - -
	(noted 1992)	1931	Liverpool	"gdVF"	£145	- - - -
	(noted 2000)	1929	Leeds	"E.F."	£390	- - - -
	(noted 1998)		Manchester	"abt.E.F."	£320	- - - -
	(noted 2001)		Manchester	£275	"gd.V.F."	- - - -
RB103	**1934 (May) K. O. Peppiatt:**					
	(noted 2001)		Hull	£500	- - - -	- - -
	(Narbeth '98)	1937	Leeds	"abt.V.F."	£220	- - - -
	(O'Grady '96)	1937	London	"gdVF"	£65	- - - -
	(noted 1993)		Liverpool	EF+	£225	- - - -
	(noted 2000)	1937	Newcastle	"gdVF"	£500	- - - -
	(Goulborn '98)		Manchester	"nr.E.F."	£165	- - - -
	(O'Grady '99)		Newcastle	"gd.Fine"	£395	- - - -

TO DIFFERENTIATE NAZI FORGERIES - See Pages 52 and 53

In Issue No. 1, Volume 31, of the I.B.N.S. Journal there is an article by Lance K. Campbell in which he states quite adamantly that there were no Operation Bernhard notes for the values £100, £500 and £1,000. As always, however, there were *other forgers* at work. Identifying a forgery does not automatically prove it to be a 'Bernhard' example. The numbers used by the Nazis for £5 notes are as follows:

A/128 to A/275 • A/281 to A/314 • A/317 to A/398
B/105 to B/131 • B/134 to B/182 • B/186 to B/237
B/256 to B/279 • J/373 to J/377

FIVE POUNDS (with metal thread)
Black and white • $8\frac{5}{16}$" x 5¼" • 211mm x 134mm
Three, same-size, serial numbers

1945 (Oct)   K. O. Peppiatt: ★

RB104	LNN	(E01 to L02)			
	(noted 1998)	E00 000000 "SPECIMEN"	"Abt.E.F."	£1,900	
		E01	£50	£80	£160
	(noted 1999)	E94	"E.F."	£75	- - - -
		H- -, J- -, K- -	£35	£60	£100
	(noted 2000)	H07	- - - -	"abt.Unc"	£110
	(noted 2000)	K01	£45	"V.F."	- - -
	(noted 1999)	K28	"E.F."	£75	- - - -
	(noted 1998)	L01 and L02	£90	£175	- - - -

★ Some notes bear a date earlier than date-of-issue

BANK OF ENGLAND NOTES

No.	Date	Signature	V.F.	E.F.	Abt. Uncirc.

FIVE POUNDS (with metal thread)
Black and white • $8\frac{5}{16}$" x $5\frac{1}{4}$" • 211mm x 134mm
Three, same-size, serial numbers

As page 52 but thinner paper and dated 1947:
1948 (Sep)

RB105	LNN	(L03 to M71)	compare with RB104		
		L03	£45	£90	£150
(noted 1998)		L-- --.--.47	---	"gd.E.F."	£75
(noted 2000)		L67	---	---	£140
(noted 1998)		M22	---	---	£90
		M71	£45	£90	£150

1949 (Dec.) P. S. Beale:

Numbers Appear: CENTRE LEFT, TOP and BOTTOM RIGHT

RB106	LNN	(M72 to Y70)			
(noted 1998)		M00 000000 "SPECIMEN"		"Abt.E.F."	£1,500
		M72	£45	£70	£125
(noted 2000)		M99	---	---	£110
		N-- to X--	£40	£60	£80
(noted 1998)		O99	£20	£65	----
(noted 1999)		X99 "nr.V.F." £45	"abt.E.F."	£70	
		Y01	---	---	£95
		Y25		"E.F." £80	----

OPERATION BERNHARD
Distinguishing "Right" from "Wrong"

The Nazis made one "improvement" to the British watermark. Possibly, they did it so that they could accurately detect their own forgeries, particularly the top quality ones. Or, perhaps, it was a cunning anti-Nazi act by the team who laid the wires in the watermarking process. Or, again, nothing more than a gentle nudge from a "tidy mind". It is the one proven indicator which distinguishes the forgery from the genuine.

A white/clear line in the watermark of the counterfeit notes points to the centre of the triangular serif at the foot of the first 'N' of ENGLAND. In genuine notes the line is off-centre and to the left of the serif when viewed the right way around. In the close-ups below, the critical parts have been intensified (don't expect this on real notes!). The "negative" at left gives a very good "picture" notwithstanding the half-linear reproduction.

BANK OF ENGLAND NOTES 53

Counterfeit Notes

Genuine Notes

"WATERMARK" WILL BE SEEN IF THIS PAGE IS HELD UP TO THE LIGHT

RB105

BANK OF ENGLAND NOTES

RB108
LNNL

RB105 watermark with boxed number 19488 · see also page 53

BANK OF ENGLAND NOTES   55

No.	Date	Signature	V.F.	E.F.	About Uncirc.

FIVE POUNDS (with metal thread) continued

Design and size as page 52

1955   L. K. O'Brien:

RB107	LNN	(Y71 to Z99)			
		Y71	£40	£90	£135
		Y--	£25	£65	£85
(Auction 1996)		"No serial number"		---	£450
		Z--	£20	£60	£80
(noted 1998)		Z33	"abt.E.F."	£65	----
(noted 1996)		Z96	---	£95	£145
(noted 2001)		Z96	"gd.Fine"	£85	---	----

RB108	LNNL	(A01A to D99A)			
		A--A	£20	£45	£75
(sundry 2000):		A01A	"gd.Fine"	£85	---	----
		A03A	"gd.V.F."	£65	---	----
		A83A	---	"abt.Unc"	£105
		A87A	"E.F."	£80	----
		B16A	"abt.E.F."	£65	----
		C78A	"E.F."	£80	----
		D75A	---	"Unc"	£140

SERIES 'B'   FIVE POUNDS
Helmeted Britannia / Lion-and-Key
Blue, green, orange • $6\frac{5}{16}$" x $3\frac{9}{16}$" • 160mm x 90mm
Back has large "Lion-and-Key" centrally

L. K. O'Brien:
1957 (Feb.)
The £5 medallions are 'solid' blue
See page 56

RB109	LNN	(A01 to E37)			
(noted 1993)	A01	(first 1500)	Low serial		£125
(Spink 1996)	A03	(first 2000)	Low serial		£45
(error 1998)	Pair with same serial		£285	"gdFine to V.F."	----
	B01, C01, D01		---	---	£40
	B--, C--, D--		£10	£20	£30
(noted 1998)	A97, B98, C97, D96		---	£35	£45
(noted 1999)	A86	"abt.V.F."	£40	patch missing print
(noted 2001)	E01 and E31		---	£35	£50

56 BANK OF ENGLAND NOTES

No.   Date   Signature   V.F.   E.F.   Uncirc.

SERIES 'B'   FIVE POUNDS
Helmeted Britannia/Lion-and-Key
Blue, green, orange • $6\frac{5}{16}$" x $3\frac{9}{16}$" • 160mm x 90mm
Back has large "Lion-and-Key" centrally

L. K. O'Brien:

    1961 (July)   £5 medallions (back) now in outline
RB110   LNN   (H01 to K45)
                    H01   - - -   £250   £350
(sundry 1999):
                    H01   "gd.V.F."   £200   - - - -
                    H02   "E.F."   £40   - - -
                    J01   - - -   "abt.Unc."   £35
                    J28   - - -   "Unc."   £35

RB109 LNN

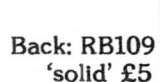

Back: RB109 'solid' £5

Back: RB110 · 'outline' £5

BANK OF ENGLAND NOTES 57

No.	Date	Signature		V.F.	E.F.	Uncirc.

SERIES 'C'   **FIVE POUNDS: Portrait**
H.M. The Queen (front) • Seated Britannia (back)
Blue • 5½" x 3 5/16" • 140mm x 84mm

1963 (Feb.)   J. Q. Hollom:

RB111	LNN	(A01 to R16)	A01	£35	£70	£120
	(noted 1996)		A00 000000 o/p 'SPECIMEN'		"EF"	£900
	Sundry 1999:		A02, A03	- - -	£25	£40
			A04, A05	- - -	£20	£30
			-01s	- - -	- - -	£40
			R16	£25	£40	£80
RB112	LNN	(M01 to M10)	Replacement note			
			M01	£70	£150	£225
			M- -	£30	£50	£75

1967 (Jan.)   J. S. Fforde:

RB113	LNN	(R20 to Z99)	R20	£30	£65	£105
	(West 1998)	"Fforde but A00 000000 SPECIMEN gd.E.F."				£1200
			R- -	£10	£20	£45
			"mids"	- - -	£12	£20
			Z99	- - -	£25	£50
RB114	LNN	(M08 to M38)	Replacement note			
			M08	£40	£90	£125
			M- -	£30	£50	£75
RB115	NNL	(01A to 40L)	01A	£40	£90	£125
			- -A	£9	£12	£20
			"mids"	- - -	£9	£18
			- -L	£25	£60	£90
RB116	NNL	(01M to 15M)	Replacement note			
	(noted 2001)		11M		"E.F." £125	- - - -
			11M	serials in sequence, per note,		£115

RB111

Illustrations are not of SPECIMEN notes. The Bank of England requires the word to be printed across all notes bearing the image of Her Majesty The Queen. (Exceptions are specified in the text.)

58 BANK OF ENGLAND NOTES

No.	Date	Signature	V.F.	E.F.	Uncirc.

SERIES 'C'   **FIVE POUNDS: Portrait**
H.M. The Queen (front) • Seated Britannia (back)
Blue • $5\frac{1}{2}$" x $3\frac{5}{16}$" • 140mm x 84mm

1971   J. B. Page:

RB117   NNL   (03C to 30L)

	03C	£10	£30	£50
	15D	"gd.E.F."	£25	---
(noted 1999)	E- -	---	"abt.Unc."	£30
	30L	£10	£25	£40
(West 2000)	Ford/Page RB115/117 75D 383485/383486			£680

RB118   NNL   (04M to 18M)   Replacement note
      (noted 1998)   11M   ---   "abt.Unc."   £140
      (noted 1998)   "Pair with consecutive serials Unc."   £350

RB115 NNL

Back: common to RB111 to RB118

BANK OF ENGLAND NOTES

| No. | Date | Signature | | V.F. | E.F. | Uncirc. |

SERIES 'D'   FIVE POUNDS : Pictorial

H.M. The Queen at right • "Winged Victory" off-centre • Britannia below.
Duke of Wellington and Battle Scene (back)
Mainly blue • 5¾" x 3$\frac{1}{16}$" • 146mm x 76mm

1971 (Nov.) J. B. Page: RB119 and RB120 were printed on
                          sheet-fed machines: 18 notes per sheet

RB119	LNN	(A01 to L94)				
	Sundry 1998:		A01	£25	£55	£80
			A--	---	---	£25
			"mids"	---	£12	£20
			L--	£15	£40	£65
			L94	---	---	£125
	(noted 1999)		Number/s written in pencil		---	£140
	(noted 2001)		Numbers printed on back		£200	"V.F."
RB120	LNN	(M01 to M05)	Replacement note			
	(noted 1999)	M01		---	"virt.Unc."	£150
	(noted 1999)	M--		---	"virt.Unc."	£125

Back: common to all from RB119 to RB128 also showing, thanks to T. I. Pett Esq., a print across a 'concertina' fold which produces a longer note with white lines when 'stretched'.

A superb example of counter pressure cylinder ink set-off.

BANK OF ENGLAND NOTES

No.   Date   Signature   V.F.   E.F.   Uncirc.

SERIES 'D'   FIVE POUNDS : Pictorial
H.M. The Queen at right • "Winged Victory" off-centre • Britannia below.
Duke of Wellington and Battle Scene (back)
Mainly blue • 5¾" x 3$\frac{1}{16}$" • 146mm x 76mm

1973 (Aug.)   J. B. Page   'L' to right of medallion (back)

RB121/124: fronts were printed direct gravure intaglio; the backs by indirect, offset, photo-lithography • on continuous reel (web) machines • 18 notes per impression.

RB121	NNL	(01A to 94Z)	01A	£25	£55	£80
			"mids"	£8	£12	£20
(noted 1998)			94Z	- - -	"Unc."	£95
(noted 2001)		"Queen looking at Wellington"			- - -	£115
(another 01)		"Queen looking at Wellington"			- - -	£125
RB122	NNL	(01M to 08M)	Replacement note			
			01M	£50	£100	£150
(noted 1998)			02M	- - -	"abt.Unc."	£130
RB123	LLNN	(AN01 to EZ56)				
			AN01	£20	£55	£80
			- -01s	- - -	£15	£30
(noted 1999)			AX07	"with differing serials"		£110
			"mids"	- - -	- - -	£20
			EZ- -	- - -	£25	£50
			EZ56	£25	£60	£85

EZ56 may be an experimental note : same prefix appears under RB124

1980 (June)   D. H. F. Somerset :

RB124	LLNN	(DN01 to LZ89 plus NA01 to NC90)				
			DN01	£32	£65	£80
(noted 1995)			DN01 000154	- - -	- - -	£195
			DN- - to DZ- -	- - -	- - -	£15
(noted 2000)			DU- -s no signature	- - -	£90	£150
			EN- - to EZ- -	- - -	- - -	£15
			HN- - to HZ- -	- - -	- - -	£15
			JN- - to JZ- -	- - -	- - -	£15
(noted 1993)			JU74 misnumbered		(E.F.+)	£55
			KN- - to LY- -	- - -	- - -	£10/£15
(noted 1993)			LX65 misnumbered sequential pair			£195
			LZ- -	- - -	£12	£25
(noted 1999)			LZ89	- - -	"Unc."	£90
			NA01	- - -	£12	£20
			NA- - to NC- -	- - -	- - -	£12
			NC90	- - -	- - -	£32

BANK OF ENGLAND NOTES 61

No.	Date		V.F.	E.F.	Uncirc.
SERIES 'D'		FIVE POUNDS : Pictorial		Details as page 60	

RB126   LL91   Serial 91 notes   (i.e. letter, letter, 91)
     sundry 1999:

		V.F.	E.F.	Uncirc.
	AN91	- - -	£395	- - - -
	BR91	- - -	- - -	- - - -
	CS91	"abt.V.F."	£250	- - - -
	DT91, EU91, HW91		- - -	- - - -
	JX91 "gd.Fine"	£85	- - -	- - - -
	KY91	- - -	£250	- - - -
	LZ91	- - -	- - -	- - - -

         1987 (July) Broader Security Thread:
RB127   LLNN   (RA01 to RC90)

(noted 1993)	RA01	low serial (first 600)			£75
(noted 1998)	RA01 000 793		- - -	- - -	£80
	RA- -, RB- -		- - -	- - -	£15
	RB01		- - -	- - -	£20
(Error 1994)	RB82 note "expands" leaving unprinted lines				£150
	RC- -		- - -	- - -	£15
(Error 1993)	RC02	V.F.+	£45	slipped	digit
(noted 1999)	RC90		- - -	- - -	£70

         1988 (March)   G. M. Gill :
RB128   LLNN (RD01 to SE90)

	RD01		- - -	- - -	£30
	RD- -		- - -	£8	£15
	RE- - to RL- -		- - -	£9	£18
(noted 1999)	RE01		- - -	- - -	£20
(noted 1999)	RK05		- - -	- - -	£24
	SA- - to SE- -				
Sundry 1999:	SB- -	seen at "Unc." £15/£18 and £20			
	SE- -		- - -	- - -	£20
	SE90		- - -	- - -	£80

RB124 · one which Mr. Somerset forgot to sign.

Series 'D' notes ceased to be legal tender as of 29th November, 1991

BANK OF ENGLAND NOTES
SERIES 'E' — FIVE POUNDS: Historical

H.M. The Queen at right • Vertical number, blue, same-size digits.
Britannia at left • Horizontal, differing-size, blue/red digits.
The back has George Stephenson at right, "Rocket" and Skerne Bridge left.
Multi-coloured • $5\frac{5}{16}$" x $2^{3}/_{4}$" • 135mm x 70mm (small variations)

First printing on Masson-Scott-Thrissell web machinery. New presses just two notes wide are to be used following tests with SNOW (Single Note On Web) equipment. £13,000,000 worth was destroyed when it was discovered that George Stephenson died 3 years later than the date shown on the notes.

1,500 wallets containing a 'last Wellington' and a 'first Stephenson' with the same serial number issued by the Bank of England @ £49.50 Printing on the web (continuous reel of paper) was, apparently, abandoned in favour of sheet printing. See RB504.

No.	Date	Signature	V.F.	E.F.	Unc..
	1990 (7th June)	G. M. Gill :			
RB129	LNN (A01 to U17)		A01	- - -	£25
	(but low serial) A02	000584	- - -	- - -	£35
	A- -; to S- -;		- - -	- - -	£9
	(noted 1999) A06	with differing serials		"Unc."	£100
	(noted 1996) E90	missing olive-green and orange			£70
	(error 1998) E67	pair consec notes missing The Queen			
	"discovered" by Colin Cockerham.				£210
	(Flashman 2000)	"Queen has blue rinse"	"gd.V.F.	£25	- - - -

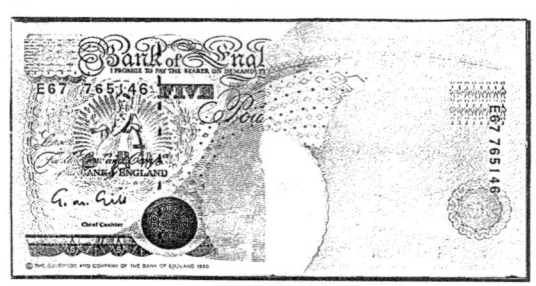

RB129 LNN consective pair missing Queen's head

BANK OF ENGLAND NOTES

No.	Date	Signature	V.F.	E.F.	Unc.

SERIES 'E'   FIVE POUNDS: Historical   Details as page 62
1991 (Nov.)   G. E. A Kentfield :

RB502	LNN	(R01 to W18)			
	(noted 1998)	R01 000024	---	---	£110
	(noted 1998)	R01 000098	---	---	£95
		R01 "mids"	---	---	£16
	(noted 2000)	S01 "mid"	---	---	£12
		W18 "High serial"	---		£75

See page 73 for £5/£10 paired serial numbers
See page 80 for £5/£20 paired serial numbers
See page 87 for £5/£10/£20/£50 matched set

RB503	LLNN	as RB502 but emboldened '£5' (AA01 to AB18)			
		These are the last web printed notes			
		AA01	---	---	£18
		AA--	---	---	£10
Three uncut notes	AB 16/7/8 999---	issue price	£39.95
(noted 1998)	AB 16/7.8 9999--	---	---	£80

1993 (March) Sheet fed 40-up
Vertical number would seem to be by a different machine/type-face:
the webb press 'pinched' A   replaced by 'normal' A

RB504	LLNN	AC01 first new sheet-fed presses			£70
Three uncut notes	AC 01/2/3 000---	issue price			£39.95
(Coincraft '94) both web and sheet uncut 3s (6 notes)			£129
	(noted 1998)	AC01/02/03	---	---	£145
		--01s	---	---	£11
	(noted 1999)	AJ-- "partial Queen's head"	£75	----
	" "	AL17 at right, AL09 at left, set of four		£295
	noted 2001)	AL--	miscut	---	£85

64 BANK OF ENGLAND NOTES
FIVE POUNDS · SERIES 'E' continued

No.	Date	Signature	Unc.

G. E. A Kentfield :

RB505 CYPHER NOTES to honour The Queen's 70th birthday
HM70 000001 to 050,000
1996 Issued in wallet together with uncirculated £5 coin £39.95

RB505

RB506 CYPHER NOTES to honour Prince of Wales 50th birthday
PW50 000001 to 001000
1998 Issued in wallet together with uncirculated £5 coin £39.95

RB506

BANK OF ENGLAND NOTES 65

Details as page 62

1998 (Jan)   Ms. Merlyn Lowther   (first woman Chief Cashier)

RB507		EA01	Uncirculated	£35
	(noted 2000)	EA01	"virt,Unc,"	£30
	DL99/EA01	Kentfield/Lowther pair issued at		£39.50

RB507

Back: series 'E'
RB129 and
RB502 to RB507

66 BANK OF ENGLAND NOTES

No.	Date	Signature	V.F.	E.F.	Abt. Unc.

TEN POUNDS
Black and white • 8¼+" x 5¼+" • 212mm x 135mm
Serial number LARGE at upper left and right
Very small repeat of number at lower right

RB151 (April 1925)   **C. P. Mahon:**
	1925	London	£100	£250	£375
(noted 1998)		Liverpool	"abtEF"	£385	- - - -
(noted 1998)	1925	Manchester	"EF+"	£450	- - - -
(noted 1999)	1927	London	"E.F."	£190	- - - -
(noted 2001)		Birmingham	"E.F."	£750	- - - -

RB152
RB152 (March 1929)   **B. G. Catterns:**
(sundry 1999)	1929	London	£100	£250	£375
(noted 1998)		Liverpool	£150	- - - -	- - - -
(noted 1998)		London	- - -	"abtUnc"	£360

RB152

BANK OF ENGLAND NOTES

No.	Date	Signature		V.F.	E.F.	Abt. Unc.

TEN POUNDS
Black and white • 8¼+" x 5¼+" • 212mm x 135mm
Serial number LARGE at upper left and right
Very small repeat of number at lower right

RB153	(August 1934)	**K. O. Peppiatt:**				
	1934	London		£125	£175	£300
(noted 1998)		London		"EF"	£185	- - - -
(1998)	28 Mar 1938	Liverpool		"E.F.+"	£300	- - - -
(1998)	17 Jan 1935	London	"GVF"	£125	"Unc"	£295
(noted 1999)		Birmingham		- - -	"abt.Unc."	£450

See Midnote Page 51: 102/K to 184/K • 187/K to 199/K
100/L to 107/L • 105/V to 153/V • 163/V to 170/V

BANK OF ENGLAND NOTES

No.   Date   Signature   V.F.   E.F.   Unc.

SERIES 'C'   **TEN POUNDS : Portrait**
Brown • $5\frac{15}{16}$" x $3^{5}/_{8}$" • 150mm x 93mm
Portrait of H. M. The Queen at right (front)
Lion with Scroll and Small Key at centre (back)

1964 (Feb)   J. Q. Hollom :
RB154   LNN   (A01 to A40)
                           A00 000000   o/p 'Specimen' twice in red
(noted 2001)   "   "   "   "abt.Unc." £1,250
                           A01   in leather folder/parchment envelope
   with Bank of England letter etc.   - - -   - - -   £1,000
                           A01   Low serial number   £30   £60
       Sundry 1998 :   A01   In sequence per note   £55
         "   "   "   A02   - - -   - - -   £48
         "   "   "   A04   - - -   £25   £50
         "   "   "   A12 etc "mids"   - - -   - - -   £30
         "   "   "   A40 with high serial   £85   "E.F."
(noted 1999)   A40   - - -   "Unc."   £115

1967 (Jan)   J. S. Fforde :
RB156   LNN   (A41 to A95)
    (noted 2001)   A00 000000   o/p 'Specimen' "E.F." £1,100   - - - -
       Sundry 2000:   A41   "abt.V.F." £65   £125
         "   "   "   A48   "low serial"   - - -   £45
         "   "   "   A81   - - -   £22   - - - -
                           A89   - - -   - - -   £45
         "   "   "   A95   - - -   "abt.Unc." £130

1971   J. B. Page :
RB158   LNN   (A91 to C88)
    (noted 1999)   A91   "virt.E.F." £900   - - - -
                           B- -   £15   £20   £35
    (error 1999)   B- - Portrait printed on back   £45   - - - -
       Sundry 1999:   C01   £18   £25   £45
         "   "   "   C48   - - -   £20   £30

		BANK OF ENGLAND NOTES			69
No.	Date	Signature	V.F.	E.F.	Unc.

SERIES 'C'   TEN POUNDS : Portrait   Details as page 68

	1971	J. B. Page :			
RB159	LNN	(M01 to M17)	Replacement note		
	(Spink 1996)	M01	- - -	"Unc"	£140
	Sundry 1999:	M01	- - -	"abt.Unc."	£110
	" " "	M07	- - -	£22	£40
	" " "	M07	- - -	"abt.Unc."	£35

RB158 LNN

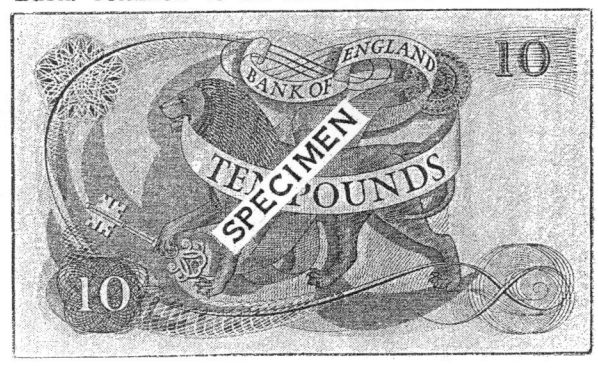

Back: common to all from RB154 to RB159

BANK OF ENGLAND NOTES

| No. | Date | Signature | V.F. | E.F. | Unc. |

SERIES 'D'   **TEN POUNDS: Pictorial**

Portrait of H. M. The Queen at right
Lily symbol centre • Britannia medallion bottom left
Florence Nightingale and Scutari scene (back)
Mainly brown • $5\frac{15}{16}$" x $3^{3/8}$" • 151mm x 85mm

1975 (Feb.)   **J. B. Page :**

RB161	LNN	(A01 to T20)			
	(noted 1996)	A00 000000			
		a specimen NOT overprinted as such			
	(noted 1998)	A00 000000 o/p SPECIMEN	"virt.Unc."		£1,500
	(noted 1999)	A01	---	£35	£160
		A--	---	£15	£35
	(error 1993)	A22 No signature		£50	£155
		B--, C--, D--, E--	£15	£20	£25
	(noted 1999)	C01	---	---	---
	(error 1993)	B30 Mirror front on back		E.F.+	£30
		H--, J--, K--, L--	£15	£20	£39
		N--, R--, S--	£15	£20	£45
	(noted 2000)	Mirror image	---	"gd.E.F."	£120
	(noted 1999)	N57	---	"abt.Unc."	£30
	(noted 1998)	T--	---	---	£30

U39   a single example reported by Duggleby
appears to be from a Page 'signatured' sheet with Somerset numbers.
(at auction 1999)   ---   ---   £632

RB161 unsigned by J. B. Page

RB162	LNN	(M01 to M50)	Rep;lacement note		
		M01	£30	£60	£90
	(noted 1998)	M01 Low serial number			£105
	(noted 1998)	M10	---	"abtUnc"	£95
		M50	£35	£75	£110
	(noted 1999)	Unspecified	---	---	£75

BANK OF ENGLAND NOTES 71

No.	Date	Signature	V.F.	E.F.	Unc.

SERIES 'D'   TEN POUNDS: Pictorial   Details as page 70

1980 (Dec.)   D. H. F. Somerset :

No.		Signature	V.F.	E.F.	Unc.
RB163	LNN	(U01 to Z80)			
		U01	£40	£100	£150
		U--	---	£20	£30
	(noted 1992)	U-- "Nightingale half-printed EF+"			£55
		W--, X--, Y--		£15	£25
		Z01	---	£25	£60
		Z80	---	£50	£100
RB164	NNL	(01A to 40L)			
		01A	---	£40	£75
		--B, --C, --D, --E		£15	£35
		--H, --J, --K,		£15	£35
		--L	---	£35	£50
		40L	---	£40	£60

1984 (Feb.)   **With small 'L'**   (between bottom left scallops)
(printed 'litho' i.e. by offset photo-lithography)

No.			V.F.	E.F.	Unc.
RB165	LLNN	(AN01 to CR90)			
	Sundry 2000:	AN01	---	£69	£115
	" " "	AN01 000021	---	---	£165
	" " "	AR-- to AZ--	---	£15	£25
	" " "	AT--	---	---	£30
	" " "	--01s	---	---	£30
		BN-- to BZ--	---	£12	£20
		CN--	---	£12	£20
		CR--	---	£14	£25
	(noted 1999)	CR--	---	---	£35
	(noted 1998)	CR90	"E.F."	£25	---

RB165 LLNN

With small 'L'

72 BANK OF ENGLAND NOTES

No.	Date	Signature	V.F.	E.F.	Unc.

SERIES 'D'   TEN POUNDS: Pictorial   Details as page 70
D. H. F. Somerset :

1987 (July)   With "Stardust" Thread :

RB166   LLNN   Exactly as RB165 but now with "broken" or 'window' ("Stardust") Security Thread (CS01 to DN30)

CS01	---	£20	£40
"mids"	---	£15	£20
CS90	---	---	£25
--01s	---	£15	£30
DN30	---	£30	£50

RB166 LLNN
with "Stardust" Thread

1988 (March)   G. M. Gill :

RB167   LLNN   (DR01 to JR60)

	DR01 Low serial		£25	£45
	DR01 High serial		---	£30
	DR--	---	---	£22
(noted 1996)	DR90	"gdVF"	£12	----
	DS-- to DZ--	---	---	£15
(noted 1999)	DU81	---	---	£89
	DW01	---	---	£30
	EN-- to EZ--	---	---	£15
Sundry 1998:	EW01	---	---	£20
" " "	EY80	---	"virt.Unc."	£20
(noted 2000)	HT01	"E.F."	£17	---
Sundry 1999:	JN01	---	£16	----
" " "	JN24	"first 500"	£30	----
" " "	JN60	---	---	£75

Kentfield number   KN52 Gill signature. See 'B, ream page 75

BANK OF ENGLAND NOTES 73

No.	Date	Signature	V.F.	E.F.	Unc.

SERIES 'D'   **TEN POUNDS: Pictorial**   Details as page 70

1991 (Nov.)   G. E. A. Kentfield :

RB168	LLNN	(KN01 to KR30)			
	Sundry 1999:	KN01	---	---	£40
	" " "	KN01 001--	---	---	£135
	" " "	KN01 000095	---	---	£160
	" " "	KN03	---	---	£30
	" " "	KN23	---	---	£15
	" " "	KN30	£40	£60	£90
	(noted 2001)	KN30	£38	---	----
	(noted 1996)	£5/£10 Pair RN01/KN01 000094			£200
		£5/£10 Pair RN01/KN01 000098			£275
		£5/£10 Pair RN01/KN01 000248			£265
	(noted 2001)	£5/£10 AA01/A01	---	---	£50

SERIES 'D' £10 ceased to be legal tender after May 20th, 1994

Example of counter pressure cylinder ink set-off or 'mirror image'

Back : Series 'D' RB161 to RB168

74 BANK OF ENGLAND NOTES
SERIES 'E' TEN POUNDS: New Portrait

More mature portrait of H. M. The Queen at right
Britannia at left with Chief Cashier's signature below
Portrait of Charles Dickens at right
Cricket Match at Dingley Dell "Pickwick Papers" at left
Multi-coloured • $5\frac{9}{16}$" x $2\frac{15}{16}$" • 142mm x 75mm

No.	Date	Signature	V.F.	E.F.	Unc.
	1992 (29th April)	**G. E. A. Kentfield :**			
RB1001	LNN	(A01 to X40)			
		A01 within first 400	---	---	£95
	(noted 1998)	A01	"first 800"		£90
	(noted 1999)	A01	---	---	£29
		"mids"	---	--- £15/£20	
		B-- to X--	---	---	£15
	(error 1993)	B80 Fine £70	"missing value etc."		
	(error 1993)	H78 "miscut"	---	£40	---
	(error 2001)	U33 "miscut"	---	"Unc."	£200
	(noted 1999)	X40 999---	---	"Unc"	£65
	£5/£10	AA01/A01 006---	---	pair	£70
	£10D/£10E	KR30/A01 matched serials	issued at		£129
(1998)	£10D/£10E	KR30/A01 matched serials	offered at		£425

RB1001 LNN "miscut"

Emboldened £10

Back : series 'E' £10
RB1001 to RB1005

BANK OF ENGLAND NOTES 75

SERIES 'E'   **TEN POUNDS: New Portrait**   Details as page 74

No.	Date		V.F.	E.F.	Unc.

RB1002   **RECLAIMED/'B' REAM NOTES**
Unspoilt notes taken from partly spoilt sheets and separately numbered. Expect 'odd' prefixes. Duggleby lists M01 to M40; Y76 to Y84 and Z-- to Z90.

(noted 1999)	M12	---	"abtUnc"	£30
(noted 1998)	Z90	---	"virt.Unc"	£40
(noted 2000)	M03 and M20	"gd.E.F." & abt.Unc." £25		£30

1993 (Nov.)   Emboldened '£10' left · also replaces crown at right

RB1003   LLNN
2000 selection

	DD01 000119	---	---	£55
	DD01 004---	---	---	£32
	DD01 000548	---	---	£40
	DE01, DR01, KB01 etc.	---	---	£25
(noted 2001	AA00 000000	---	"abt.Unc"	£1,100

RB1004   **CYPHER NOTES:**   to mark H.M. The Queen's 70th birthday
HM70 000001 to 002000
Issued as cased set of NOTE plus Silver Proof £5 coin   £97.50

RB1005   **CYPHER NOTES:**   to mark the Prince of Wales 50th birthday
PW50 000001 to 000500
Issued as cased set of NOTE plus Silver Proof £5 coin   £97.50

RB1004 Serial HM70------

RB1005 Serial PW50------

76
SERIES 'E'

BANK OF ENGLAND NOTES
TEN POUNDS: New Portrait

More mature portrait of H. M. The Queen at right
Britannia at left with Chief Cashier's signature below
Portrait of Charles Dickens at right
Cricket Match at Dingley Dell "Pickwick Papers" at left
Multi-coloured • $5\frac{9}{16}$" x $2\frac{15}{16}$" • 142mm x 75mm

No.	Date	Signature	V.F.	E.F.	Unc.
	1999 (January)	**Ms. Merlyn Lowther :**			
RB1006	LLNN	KL01	- - -	- - -	£40
	(noted 2001)	KL01	- - -	"virt.Unc."	£39
		LA01	- - -	- - -	£20
		LL- -	- - -	- - -	£45
	KK99/KL01	Kentfield/Lowther serial pairs issued			£54.95

RB1006 LLNN

Back : series'E' RB1006

BANK OF ENGLAND NOTES

SERIES 'E'   **TEN POUNDS: New Portrait**

Large £10 at left · H. M. The Queen at right · small 10 (no £ sign)
Britannia hologram at left with Chief Cashier's signature beside
Back: Magnifying Glass/Bird at left · Portrait of Charles Darwin at right

Multi-coloured • $5\frac{9}{16}$" x $2\frac{15}{16}$" • 142mm x 75mm

No.	Date	Signature	V.F.	E.F.	Unc.
	2000 (7th Nov.) Ms. Merlyn Lowther :				
RB1007	LLNN		---	---	---
	(noted 2001)	AA01 007---	---	"Unc"	£15

RB1007 LLNN

Back : series'E' RB1007

BANK OF ENGLAND NOTES

No.	Date	Signature	V.F.	E.F.	About Uncirc.

TWENTY POUNDS

Black and white • $8\frac{5}{16}$" x $5\frac{5}{16}$" • 212mm x 135mm
Serial number LARGE at upper left and upper right
Very small repeat of number at lower right

1925 to 1929   C. P. Mahon :
RB171   £400   £800   - - - -

1929 to 1934   B. G. Catterns :
RB172   £350   £675   - - - -
    (noted 2001)   "E.F."   £750   - - - -

1934   K. O. Peppiatt :
RB173   £350   £675   - - - -
    (noted 2001)   "E.F."   £650   - - - -
    (noted 2001)   49/M   presumed genuine   £725   - - - -
                                                    (see below)

These three are rarely encountered. Valuations without 'market movements' are "guesstimates". Valuations presume London notes; branch notes will attract a substantial premium.
See mid-note page 51 · 43/M to 55/M

RB172 Filmed as genuine, further examination (page 53) indicates a forgery

BANK OF ENGLAND NOTES

SERIES 'D' — TWENTY POUNDS: Pictorial

Portrait of H. M. The Queen at right with
St. George-and-The-Dragon centre • Britannia medallion at left.
Watermark: Queen Elizabeth II
The back has a statue of Shakespeare at right • "Romeo and Juliet" at left
Mainly purple • $6^{1}/_{4}$" x $3^{1}/_{2}$" • 160mm x 90mm

No.	Date	Signature		V.F.	E.F.	About Uncirc.
	1970 (July)	**J. S. Fforde :**				
RB174	LNN	(A01 to A05)				
	Sundry 1999:		A01	£80	£140	- - - -
	„ „ „		A03	- - -	"abt.Unc."	£95
	„ „ „		A04	- - -	"Unc."	£145
RB175	Replacement		M01 (only)	£80	£180	£250
	(noted 1999)		M01	- - -	"abt.Unc"	£250
	1970	**J. B. Page :**				
RB176	LNN	(A06 to D79)				
			A06	£80	£150	£225
	(noted 1999)		A09	- - -	"abt.Unc"	£60
	(error 2001)		A- -	"missing	colours Unc."	£180
	Sundry 20000		B- -, C- -	- - -	- - -	£55
	„ „		C57 "mirror	image abt.E.F."	£85	- - - -
	„ „		D01	- - -	£39	- - - -
	„ „		D- -	- - -	£29	£50
RB177	LNN	(M01 to M04)		Replacement note		
	Sundry 1999:					
	„ „		M01	£60	£95	£165
	„ „		M03	- - -	- - -	£93
	„ „		M04	- - -	£75	- - - -

Back : series 'D' £20
RB174 to RB181

BANK OF ENGLAND NOTES
SERIES 'D' — TWENTY POUNDS
Details as page 79

No.	Date	Signature	V.F.	E.F.	Unc.

1981 (March) D. H. F. Somerset :

RB178	LNN	(E01 to J40)	E01, H-- and J-- to J40		
		E01	£45	£100	£150
	(noted 1998)	E06	---	---	£85
	" "	E--	---	£40	£70
	" "	J40	---	£50	£80
	(noted 1999)	No prefix, no serial numbers			£200
	(noted 2001)	H03	"E.F."	£45	----

1984 (Nov.) Watermark changed to image of Shakespeare. "Stardust" (window) security thread introduced.

RB180	NNL	(01A to 40K)			
	(noted 1998)	01A 000585		---	£185
	Sundry 2001:	01A 000072	---	---	£195
	" "	01A	"E.F."	£85	----
	" "	55D	---	---	£40
	" "	17H "error pair differing numbers			£350
	" "	01K	---	£65	£80
	" "	30K	---	---	£70
	" "	40K	---	£50	£75
	"Queen's head missing front 'mirrored' back			£120	----

1988 (March) G. M. Gill :

RB181	NNL	(01L to 20X)			
		01L	£25	£45	£70
	(noted 1998)	01L 930000		---	£105
	(noted 1999)	20L	---	£24	----
	Error: successive pair, one missing much detail				£135
	Error: ink 'set off' reversed back onto front				£135
	(noted 1994) Error: "numbers upside down"			---	£325
	(noted 1999)	05T "extra paper at bottom left"			£175
	(noted 1999) "extra paper, missing serial"			£180	----
	(noted 2001)	01M	---	£25	£60
	(error 2001)	22R missing detail from both sides			£395
	Sundry 2001:	55T concertina fold (see pic RB127)			£95
	" "	73T	---	---	£50
	" "	10U	---	£35	£50
	" "	--X	---	£35	£50
	(noted 1998)	20X	---	"abt.Unc."	£150

RB128/RB181
£5D/£20D SE68/20U matched serials issued at £117.50
£5D/£20D SE68/20U matched serials offered at £300

SERIES 'D'
BANK OF ENGLAND NOTES
TWENTY POUNDS
81
Details as page 79

RB180 counter pressure cylinder ink set-off causing 'mirror image'

RB181 missing much detail

RB181 · NNL
10U 'fun' prefix

82
SERIES 'E'

BANK OF ENGLAND NOTES
TWENTY POUNDS

Portrait of H. M. The Queen at right
Britannia at left, cashier's signature below

Michael Faraday at right • Scene from a Faraday demonstration at left
Multi-coloured • 5⁷/₈" x 3¹/₈" • 148/149mm x 79/80 mm

No.	Date	Signature	V.F.	E.F.	Unc.
	1991 (5th June) G. M. Gill :				
RB182	LNN	(A01 to S07)			
	(Noted 2001)	A01 00000-	---	"Unc."	£500
	Sundry 2000:	A01 001---	---	---	£60
	" "	A01 consecutive pair	---		£100
	" "	A01 006---	---	---	£55
	" "	-01s	---	---	£42
	" "	A27 and B27 on same note "nr.E.F."		£110	----
	(Spink 1996)	"Missing print above Queen's head abtUnc"			£120
	(noted 2001)	"Missing Queen's head abt.Unc."	---		£125
	(noted 2001)	unspecified mismatched serials	"Unc."		£125
		A65 Spectacular miscut affecting two notes			
	(noted 2000)	and missing numbers at right "E.F"	£225		----
	£20D/£20E	20X/A01 matched serials		Issued	£194

RB2001 'B' REAM: unspoilt notes taken from partly spoilt sheets and separately numbered. The prefixes are outside the 'normal' range (others would be difficult to identify).

Sundry quotes:	A78		"EF+"	£40	----
" "	A91		"abtEF"	£50	----
" "	B84	"gdVF"	£24	---	----
" "	B90		---	abtUnc	£60
" "	Z30		---	abtUnc	£40

Back : series 'E' £20
RB182 and
RB2001 to RB2005

BANK OF ENGLAND NOTES
SERIES 'E'   TWENTY POUNDS   83
Details as page 82

RB182 Spectacular miscut

No.	Date	Signature	V.F.	E.F.	Unc.
RB2002	1991 (25th Nov.) LNN	G. E. A. Kentfield : (E01 to W35)			
		Uncut pair (1,000 only) Issue price			£75
	Sundry 1999:	E01 001---	---	---	£110
	" "	E01 001067	---	---	£80
	" "	E01	---	---	£69
	" "	E52	---	£20	----
	" "	R01	---	---	£40
	(Notability '96)	E17 "Queen's head missing VF+"			£60
	(Goulborn '01)	N-- "part of next note at right"			£125
	(White 1996)	S01	---	"Unc."	£35
	(Mason 1996)	W29 "Miscut, missing lower print gdVF"			£25
	(noted 2001)	W35 999---	---	---	£85
	1995 (Oct)	E01/E02/ 000001 to 00100 Uncut Pairs £108.28			

BANK OF ENGLAND NOTES
SERIES 'E' — TWENTY POUNDS

No.	Date	Signaturw	V.F.	E.F.	Unc.

RB2003 LNN   G. E. A. Kentfield   Design Change (X01 to Y70)
Front · £20 at left emboldened · crown at right replaced by £20
Back · £20 at left in new style · £20 added at right · 'richer' colour

(Goulborn '01)	X01 0010--	---	"Unc."	£75
(Coincraft '93)	X01 "first 1500"	---	---	£38.50
Sundry 1999:	X01 001023	---	---	£75
" "	X30	---	---	£30
" "	Y01	---	---	£45
" "	Y70	---	---	£60

RB2004 LLNN   (AA01 etc.)

(noted 2001)	AA01	---	"abt.Unc."	£95
	--01s	---	---	£30/£40
(O' Grady '94)	AB64 "error: extra paper gd.VF/EF"			£135
(error 19980	"3 sequential (2 minus thread)"			£250
(error 1999)	"no numbers at right"	---		£180
(noted 2001)	AB-- 349789/549789 same note			£145

1999 (Jan.)   Ms. Merlyn Lowther   first woman Chief cashier
RB2005 LLNN

	DA01	---	---	£70
(noted 2001)	DA80	---	---	£75
CL99/DA01	Kentfield/Lowther serial pair			£89.50

RB2006 LLNN   Design Change
Large £20 at left · back: Edward Elgar and Worcester Cathedral

	AA01	---	---	£40

RB2006 LLNN

Elgar and Worcester Cathedral

BANK OF ENGLAND NOTES
FIFTY POUNDS

Black and white • $8\frac{5}{16}$" x $5\frac{5}{16}$" • 212mm x 135mm
Serial number LARGE at upper left and upper right
Very small repeat of number at lower right

No.	Date	Signature		V.F.	E.F.	E.F.+ Abt.Unc.
RB191	1925 to 1929	C. P. Mahon :		£425	£825	- - - -
RB192	1929 to 1934	B. G. Catterns :		£325	£625	- - - -
RB193	1934	K. O. Peppiatt :		£300	£500	£700
	(Mason 1996)		£105		"Fine, few small holes"	
	(noted 1998)		- - -	"E.F."	£450	
	" "		- - -	- - - -	"gd.EF"	£600
	(G. & J. White)		- - -	"gd.V.F."	£360	- - - -
	(noted 1998)	57/N	- - -	"E.F."	£750	- - - -
	(Goulborn '01)	Liverpool	- - -	"backstamped"		£750
Skit Note "Swank of England . . . . . 50 rounds					£30	- - - -

See mid-note page 51 · 42/N to 61/N

RB193

BANK OF ENGLAND
FIFTY POUNDS

SERIES 'D'   Portrait of H. M. The Queen.   **PICTORIAL**
A Phoenix centre • Cathedral design detail off-centre.
Britannia medallion at lower left.
back: Sir Christopher Wren and St Paul's Cathedral
Multicoloured • 6⁷/₈" x 3³/₄" • 169mm x 95mm
The security thread is serrated along one edge.
This ragged edge falls randomly to right or left.

No.	Date	Signature	V.F.	E.F.	Uncirc.

1981 (Mar.)   **D. H. F. Somerset** :

RB194	LNN	(A01 to B90)			
	(noted 1999)	A01 001--	---	"abtUnc"	£175
	Sundry 2000:	A01	---	"abtUnc"	£120
	" "	B90	---	£75	£100
	" "	B90	"High serial number"		£175
	" "	"mids"	---	£60	£80
	Error	Buildings missing (below cathedral)		£150	----
	Error	Upper serial number missing	---	---	£200

1988   **G. M. Gill:**
"Stardust" ('windowed') security thread. Spot-colour changes.

RB195	LNN	(C01 to D90)			
		C01	£60	£95	£130
		C--; D--;	---	£65	£95
		D22 Queen's peers out above St.Paul's			£200
		D90	£60	£95	£130

Gill signed prefixes 'D' & 'E' exist to replace spoilt Kentfields
thus (noted 1998) D95   "E.F."   £90   ----

Set: £10 'D'/£50 'D' Issued at £130 + VAT
(Narbeth'95) £5/£20/£50   000054/001054/000054   £450

BANK OF ENGLAND
FIFTY POUNDS

No.	Date	Signature	V.F.	E.F.	Uncirc.
	1991 (25th Nov.) G. E. A. Kentfield :				
RB196	LNN	(E01 to E30)			
	(noted 1998)	E01	---	---	£100
	" "	E01	---	---	£145
	" "	E02 000006	---	"abt.Unc."	£165
		E30 High serial		---	£200

(noted '98) Set: £5/£10/£50 R01/A01/E01 matching serials £350
Set : £5/£10/£20/£50 - 500001 to 502000 - issued at £175 + VAT
(West 1998) £5/£10/£20/£50 "All A01 000713" £400
(noted 1998) £5/£10/£20/£50 R/KN/E/E01 500--- £300

RB196 LNN

Back:
RB194, 195 & 196

BANK OF ENGLAND
FIFTY POUNDS

SERIES 'E'   H. M. The Queen   **HISTORICAL**

silver foil Tudor rose · silver foil medallion · vertical number impinges on rose
back: Sir John Houblon, first Governor of the Bank of England
His house in Threadneedle Street · Vignette of Gate-keeper
Multicoloured · 3⁵/₁₆ x 6³/₁₆ · 85mm x 156mm

No.	Date	Signature	V.F.	E.F.	Unc.
	1994 (20th April) G. E. A. Kentfield :				
RB5001	LNN				
(noted 1998)		A01 000808	- - -	- - -	£150
"	"	A01 010000	- - -	- - -	£135
Sundry 2000:		A01 003400	- - -	"abt.Unc."	£95
"	"	A01 999967	- - -	- - -	£95
"	"	L06 and L07 same serial pair	- - -		£285
"	"	"shark's fin and missing cypher"	£200		- - - -
"	"	"extra paper at left abt.E.F."	£140		- - - -
"	"	M99	- - -	- - -	£150
(G.&J.White '99)		£10/£50 "Both A01 000515"			£200

1,500 wallets Last 'D'/ First 'E' E30/A01 998500 - 999999

RB5002	LNN	"B" REAM (see page 82)			
(noted 1998)		A99	- - -	"abt.Unc."	£100
Sundry 2000:		A99	- - -	- - -	£105
"	"	A99	- - -	£75	- - - -
"	"	C01	- - -	- - -	£95
"	"	D94	- - -	"Unc."	£140

RB5001 LNN

BANK OF ENGLAND

SERIES 'E'   FIFTY POUNDS   Design as page 88

| No. | Date | Signature | V.F. | E.F. | Unc. |

G. E. A. Kentfield :

RB5003   LLNN   CYPHER NOTE to mark 50th birthday Prince of Wales
PW50 000001 to PW50 000100
Issued with 22 carat gold five pounds   £895
With the gold coin being issued at £595, this makes the note £300

RB5003

1999 (January)   Ms. Merlyn Lowther :
RB5004   LNN
H99/J01 Kentfield/Lowther serial pair issued at £179.95
J01   - - -   - - -   £95

Full set Lowther notes £5/£10/£20/£50   EA/KL/DA/J01   £280

Back:
RB5001, RB5002
RB5003, RB5004

BANK OF ENGLAND NOTES

Black and white • 8$\frac{5}{16}$" x 5$\frac{5}{16}$" • 212mm x 135mm
Serial number LARGE at upper left and upper right
Very small repeat of number at lower right

No.	Date	Signature	V.F.	E.F.	About Uncirc.
		ONE HUNDRED POUNDS			
	1925 to 1929	C. P. Mahon :			
RB201			£700	£1200	- - - -
	1929 to 1934	B. G. Catterns :			
RB202			£400	£925	- - - -
	(noted 1996)	1929 GVF "restored corners"		£900	- - - -
	1934	K. O. Peppiatt :			
RB203			£325	£700	- - - -
	(noted 1996)	"VF, 2 small holes"	£250	- - - -	- - - -
	(noted 1996)	London	- - - -	£650	- - - -
	(noted 1999)	Liverpool	£975	- - - -	- - - -
	(noted 1999)	London	- - - -	"tiny repair"	£700
	(noted 2001)	Liverpool "backstamped"		£750	- - - -

Liverpool 29th Septr. 1936 · Filmed to show watermark

RB203

BANK OF ENGLAND NOTES
Details as page 90

No.	Date	Signature	V.F.	E.F.	About Uncirc.

TWO HUNDRED POUNDS
1925 to 1928   C. P. Mahon :
RB220   exists only as a specimen   guesstimate   £4000   - - - -

FIVE HUNDRED POUNDS
1925 to 1929   C. P. Mahon :
RB221   £5000   £7000   - - - -

1929 to 1934   B. G. Catterns :
RB222   £4000   £6000   - - - -
(Spink 1994) Liverpool 37Z 01717   - - - -   - - - -   £14,740

1934   K. O. Peppiatt :
RB223   £3750   £5750   - - - -
(noted 1990) Sept. 30 1936   Spinks   £5720   - - - -

ONE THOUSAND POUNDS
1925 to 1929   C. P. Mahon :
RB301   £6000   £9000   - - - -

1929 to 1934   B. G. Catterns :
RB302   £6000   £9000   - - - -

1934   K. O. Peppiatt :
RB303   £7500   £9750   - - - -

FIVE THOUSAND POUNDS
"Little is known about them at the moment" reports *Colin Narbeth* in an article in the monthly magazine "COIN NEWS". The issue may have been for use by the S.A.S.

FIFTEEN THOUSAND POUNDS
Yes. Notes for £15,000 ! Incorrectly spelt PROMISORY NOTE for use by British airmen on active service in the Gulf War. Payment of such sum to be paid to the bearer provided no harm befell the issuer (the airman). Source *Colin Narbeth* "COIN NEWS".

COLLECTORS BANKNOTES
PLATE SIZES

Throughout a major print run some variations occur, either to the size of the plate used or, more likely, to the design borne by the plate. In most instances the values of the resulting banknotes are unaffected. Those variations which do affect the values are set out here. Any old ruler will do to detect a *difference in size* of the printed images, but a stainless steel printer's rule is necessary to determine a precise measurement. A small reduction, less then 0.5mm when compared with the 'norm', might well be due to paper shrinkage.

RB7 and RB8 · page 20

Plate/design No.1 Total length of print = 126mm Plate/design No.2 Total length of print = 128mm   For No.2 add 25% to values.

With top edge of metric scale at top of the letters forming the words "Ten Shillings" (centre of note) the distance from curve at left (Maclise Britannia) to the outermost curve at right (value tablet) will be found to be 126mm on the majority of notes.

RB14 · page 21

Plate/design No.1 Total length of print = 126mm
Plate/design No.2 Total length of print = 127mm
Plate/design No.3 Total length of print = 129mm

Following further researh, these sizes are different from those given in earlier editions. We believe it will be found that there is a visible colour difference which invites further examination.

For No.2 add 20% to values, and for No.3 add 40%.

Plate/design Variations for the Britannia Pound

RB36 Peppiatt	Total length of print	139mm
RB42 Peppiatt (blue)	Total length of print	141mm
RB46 Peppiatt	Total length of print	142.5mm
RB51 Beale	Total length of print	142mm

The ornate word "One" and the Cashier's signature are set on a long, green or or blue rectangle. The length of that rectangle is the one to verify.

JOIN THE I.B.N.S. !
Membership due in U.S.$ and U.K. £s

Regular Membership	$20.00	£12.50	
Family Membership	$25.00	£15.50	
Junior Membership	$10.00	£6.00	
Life Membership	$400.00	£250.00	
Euro cheques add		.50	

Cheque and application to:

Milan Alusic   Mrs. Sally Thowney
P.O. Box 1642   36 B
Racine   Dartmouth Park Hill
Wisconsin 53401 London · NWS 1HN
U.S.A   U.K.

COLLECTORS BANKNOTES
BIBLIOGRAPHY

"As Good As Gold"	Virginia Hewitt/John Keyworth	British Museum Publications
"Bank of England and Treasury Notes"	D. M. Miller	Corbitt & Hunter Ltd
"Coin News" - Monthly magazine		Token Publishing Ltd
"Discovering Banknotes"	Kenneth R. Lake	Shire Publications
"English Paper Money"	Vincent Duggleby	Spink & Son Ltd
"Nazi Counterfeiting of British £ Currency"		Bryan Burke
"Numismatic Circular"		Spink & Son Ltd
"Promises to Pay"	Derrick Byatt © Bank of England	Spink & Son Ltd
"The Money Makers"	W. Kranister	Blackbear Publishing
"The Story of Money"	Whitehead/Baskerville	Usborne Publishing
"The Story of Paper Money"	Yasha Beresiner/Colin Narbeth	David & Charles Ltd
"World Paper Money"	Albert Pick	Krause Publications

GRADING

Just as with coins, grading of banknotes often comes down to a matter of personal opinion. To get a great measure of agreement, however, one can use, as a first step, the "straddle". It is usually possible to get whole-hearted agreement with an approach like "well, it is certainly better than FINE but, clearly, it couldn't be called EXTREMELY FINE". Where agreement to this would be gained a statement that "this item is VERY FINE" night well have the opposite effect. After "the straddle" all that remains is to define he in-between grade and, perhaps, differ only on a plus or minus 'shading'. Is a superb example better than an uncirculated one?

A PENALTY POINT SYSTEM TO ASSIST GRADING

Deduct from 100% the following:

HOLES	Each pin hole	5 points	larger holes 10 points
EDGES	'Fluffed' or unsharp portions		5 points
	Tears short of design		10 points
	Tears reaching into design		20 points
FOLDS	Very minor 'cahier's bend'		2 points
	Discernable, unsharp fold		5 points
	Sharp, distinct crease		10 points
	Several folds (waistcoat pocket)		20 points
DIRT	Just noticeable discolouration		5 points
and	Grubbibess - Cashier marks		10 points
WEAR	Illegibility from dirt or wear		20 points
GENERAL IMPRESSION	for anything that makes you less than happy and and has not previously been penalised		1 to 5 points

Range FINE 50%; VERY FINE 75%; E.F. ANYTHING FROM 90% TO 99%

COLLECTORS BANKNOTES
LIST OF BANKNOTE DEALERS

AMCASE - Box 5376 - Akron - Ohio - OH 44313 - U.S.A.
BANKING MEMORABILIA - P.O.Box 14 - Carlisle - CA3 8DZ
BARDWELL - 7 Granary Close - Wheathampstead - 1AL 8BA
D. G. BARNEY - Greenfield - Colyton Hill - Colyton - EX24 6HY
BARRETT - Box 9 - Victoria Station - Montreal - H3Z 2V4
S. BASHOVER - P.O.Box 241 - Maplewood - NJ 07040 - U.S.A.
Y. BERESINER - 43 Templars Crescent - London - NC3 3QR
M. BLACKBURN · Box 33917 · Vancouver · B.C. · Canada V6J 4L7
B. BOSWELL · 24 Townsend Lane · Upper Boddington · Northants
C. A. BOWEN - 107 Glanymor Street - Briton Ferry - SA11 2LG
E. J. & C. A. BROOKS · 44 Kiln Rd · Thundersly · S. Benfleet · S57 1TB
Iain BURN - 2 Compton Gardens - Camberley - Surrey - GU15 2SP
M. J. CARPENTER - 10 Linden Grove - Chorley - Lancs - U.K.
COINCRAFT - 45 Great Russell Street - London - WC1B 3LU
James D. COOK · 23 Reforne · Easton · Portland · DT5 2AL
CORBITT'S - 5 Mosley Street - Newcastle-upon-Tyne - NE1 1YE
DENLY'S/BOSTON - P.O.Box 1010 - Boston - MA 02205 - U.S.A.
Clive DENNETT - 66 St. Benedicts Street - Norwich - NR2 4AR
DOLPHIN COINS · 2 Englands Lane · Hampstead · NW3 4TG · U.K.
Educational Coin Co. - Box 3826 - Kingston NY 12401 U.S.A.
EL DORADO - E.Commerce - San Antonio - Texas - U.S.A.
Steve EYER - PO Box 321 - Mount Zion - Ill 62549 U.S.A.
Chalet FLANDRIA - CH.3981 - Bitsch VS - Switzerland.
Richard FLASHMAN · 54 Ebbsfleet Walk · Gravesend · DA11 9EW
B. FRANK - 3 South Avenue - Ryton - Tyne & Wear - NE40 3LD
J. FUGATE · 3155 Commanche CT. · N.W. · Salem · Oregon · U.S.A.
FURMAN · Box 60 · Ixelles 6 · B1060 · Brussels · Belgium
GLANCE BACK Books - 17 Upper Church St. - Chepstow - Gwent
K. GOULBORN - 12 Sussex Street - Rhyl - Clwyd - U.K.
GRANTHAM COINS - P.O. Box 60 - Grantham - Lincolnshire
HENDERSON - Box 73037 - Puyallup - Washington - U.S.A.
M. T. HOBSON - Zevenaar Strasse 13 - 6290 Weilberg W.Germany
HORWEDEL - P.O.Box 2395 - West Lafayette - IN 47906 - U.S.A.
Christine HOWE - P.O.Box 3195 - London - E12 6HX
B. HUDSON - 71 The Stitch - Friday Bridge - Cambs - PE14 0HY
Peter IRELAND · 31 Clifton Street · Blackpool · FY1 1JQ
JAK - 31 Vapron Road - Mannamead - Plymouth - Devon - U.K.
The JAMES Group - 33 Timberhill - Norwich - NR1 3LA - U.K.
Richard JEFFERY · Trebehor · Porthcurno · Penzance · TR19 66X
A. JUSTUS - P.O.Box 1229 - CH-8034 - Zurich - Switzerland
Essie KASHANI - Box 8374 - Rowland Heights - Cal - U.S.A.

COLLECTORS BANKNOTES
LIST OF BANKNOTE DEALERS

KRACOV - Box 15555 - Kenmore Station - Boston - MA 02215 U.S.A.
M. LAWING - P.O.Box 9494 - Charlotte - N.C. - 28299 - U.S.A.
R. K. LODHA - Dept. B - GPO Box 3609 - Kathmandu 7107 - Nepal
R. M. LUBBOCK - 315 Regent Street - London - W1R 7YB
MARSHALL - Box 5865 - Station A - Toronto - Ontario - M5W 1P5
D. MASON - 35/36 Broad Street - Canterbury - Kent - U.K.
M. MORRIS - Box 201536 - Minneapolis - MN - 55420 - U.S.A.
Peter MORRIS · P.O. Box 223 · Bromley · Kent · BR1 4EQ · U.K.
MUSSER - Box 305 - Ridge Manor - Florida - 33525 - U.S.A.
Colin NARBETH - 6 Hall Place Gardens - St.Albans - AL1 3SP
NOTABILITY - Mallards - Chirton - Devizes - Wilts SN10 3QX
NOTAPHILIC Holland - Box 10165 - 2501HD - The Hague Holland
NOTES/AFRICA - Box 91086 - Pasadena - CA 91109 - U.S.A.
J. NUNKO - P.O. Box 1018 - Port Louis - Mauritius
Michael O'GRADY · 9/11 Kensington High Street · London W8 5NP
J.OLDIS · Wells Collectors Centre · Mill STreet · Wells · Somerset · BA5 2AS
OSVALDO - Box 9087 - 80,000 - Curitba-PR - Brazil
PENTLAND - 92 High Street - Wick - Caithness - Scotland
John PETTIT - GPO Box 4593 - Sydney 2001 - Australia
PHILLIPS · 101 · New Bond Street · London W1Y 0AS
PONTERIO - 3823 Park Blvd - Box 33588 - San Diego - CA 92103
Beate RAUCH - P.O.Box 2830 - Los Angeles - CA - 90078-2830
Clyde REEDY - P.O.Box 6638 - Marietta - GA 30065 - U.S.A.
ROGERSON - 35 Castle Street - Reading - RG1 7SB
Bill ROSEDALE · 17 Priory Close · Abbots Park · CH1 4BX · U.K.
Mike SCRIMSHAW · 13 East Avenue · Kettering · Northants · NN15 7AD
J. E. SELLARS - P.O.Box 173 - Bristol - BS99 7NW - U.K
T. SEXTON · 19 Gt.Western Av. · Bridgend · Mid Glam. · CF31 1AA
John SMITH · 47 The Shambles · York · YO1 2LX
SOTHEBY'S - Bloomfield Place - New Bond Street - London W1
SPINK & SON - 5,6,7, King St. - St.James's - London SW1Y 6QS
STEINBERG - Box 752 - San Anselmo - CA 94960 - U.S.A.
TAUNTON STAMPS - 66 Bridge Street - Taunton - Somerset - U.K.
M. VEISSID - Hobsley House - Frodesley - Shrews - SY5 7HD
WEST Promotions - P.O.Box 257 - Sutton - Surrey - SM3 9WW
George WHITE - 29 Shortacre - Basildon - Essex - SS14 2LR
W.H.COLLECTables · 500 Chesham Hse. · 150 Regent St. · W1R 5FA

RICHARD DUGGLEBY PICK

TREASURY

ONE SHILLING
RT1	T23	------
RT2	T29	P111A

HALF-CROWN
RT3	T22	
RT4	T28	P112

FIVE SHILLINGS
RT5	T21	------
RT6	T27	P112A

TEN SHILLINGS
RT7	T8	
RT8	T9	
RT8a	----	} P105
RT9	T10	
RT10	T12/1	
RT11	T12/2	
RT12	T12/3	} P107
RT13	T13/1	
RT14	T13/2	
RT15	T15 TURKEY PM1	
RT16	T17	
RT17	T18	} P109a
RT18	T19	
RT19	T20	} P109b
RT20	T25	
RT21	T26	} P113
RT22	T30	P115
RT23a	T33	P117
RT23b	T33a	------

ONE POUND
RT25a.	T1	
RT25b.		
RT25c.		
RT26a	T2	
RT26b		
RT26c		
RT27a	T3	
RT27b		P106
RT27c		
RT27d		
RT28a	T4	
RT28b		
RT29a	T5/3	
RT29b	T5/4	
RT30	T6	
RT31	T7	
RT32	T11/1	} P108
RT33	T11/2	
RT34	T14 TURKEY PM2	
RT35	T16	P110
RT36	T24	P114
RT36a	----	------
RT37	T31	P116
RT38	T32	------
RT39	T34	P118
RT40	T35	------

RICHARD 2001 11th
"Collectors Banknotes"

DUGGLEBY
"English Paper Money" 5th

BANK of ENGLAND

HALF-CROWN
RB1	B254	P121

FIVE SHILLINGS
RB2	B253	P122

TEN SHILLINGS
RB3	B210	P119a
RB5	B223	P119b
RB7	B235	
RB8	B236	} P119c
RB10	B251	P123
RB12	B256	P119d
RB14	B262	P126a
RB15	B263	----
RB16	B265	
RB17	B266	} P126b
RB18	B267	----
RB19	B271	P126c
RB20	B272	----
RB21	B286	P130a
RB22	B287	----
RB23	B294	
RB24	B295	} P130b
RB25	B296	----
RB26	B309	
RB27	B310	} P130c
RB28	B311	----

ONE POUND
RB31	B212	P120a
RB33	B225	P120b
RB34	B226	----
RB36	B238	P120c
RB37	B239	
RB38	B240	
RB31a	B212(A)	P120e
RB33a	B225(A)	P120f
RB34a	B226(A)	
RB36a	B238(A)	P120g
RB37a	B239(A)	
RB37b	B239(B)	P120h
RB37c	B239(C)	
RB41	B248	
RB42	B249	} P124a
RB44	B258	P120d
RB46	B260	P127a
RB47	B261	----
RB51	B268	P127b
RB52	B269	----
RB53	B273	P127c
RB54	B274	----

PICK
"Standard Catalogue of World Paper Money" 7th
The 8th edition has 7th edition numbers in brackets beside each new number.

At the time of going to press, we believe these comparisons to be accurate. They are presented as an aid to ready reference and have been updated to incorporate changes made known to us. No responsibility is taken, however, should there be changes to catalogue numbers. We shall endeavour not to change Richard numbers.

BANK of ENGLAND

ONE POUND
RB61	B281	
RB62	B282	
RB63R	B283	} P131a
RB64	B284	
RB65	B285	
RB66	B288	
RB67	B289	
RB68	B290	} P131b
RB69	B291	
RB70G	B292	
RB71G	B293	
RB72	B301	
RB73	B302	
RB74G	B303	
RB75G	B304	} P131c
RB76	B305	
RB77	B306	
RB78G	B307	
RB79G	B308	
RB81	B320	
RB82	B321	
RB83	B322	} P131d
RB84	B323	
RB85	B337	
RB86	B338	
RB87	B339	} P137a
RB87E	B339a	
RB88	B340	
RB89	B341	
RB90	B342	} P137b

FIVE POUNDS
RB101	B215	P79
RB102	B228	P87
RB103	B241	P94
RB104	B255	P101
RB105	B264	P102
RB106	B270	P103
RB107	B275	
RB108	B276	} P104
RB109	B277	P128
RB110	B280	P129
RB111	B297	
RB112	B298	} P132a
RB113	B312	
RB114	B313	
RB115	B314	} P132b
RB116	B315	
RB117	B324	
RB118	B325	} P132c
RB119	B332	
RB120	B333	
RB121	B334	
RB122	B335	} P135a
RB123	B336	
RB124	B343	P135b
RB126	B344	
RB127	B345	
RB128	B353	P135d
RB129	B357	P139
RB502	B361	P139c
RB503	B362	P142
RB504	B363	
RB505		
RB506		
RB507		

BANK of ENGLAND

TEN POUNDS
RB151	B216	P80
RB152	B229	P88
RB153	B242	P95
RB154	B299	
RB155	B300	} P133a
RB156	B316	
RB157	B317	} P133b
RB158	B326	
RB159	B327	} P133c
RB161	B330	
RB162	B331	} P136a
RB163	B346	
RB164	B347	} P136b
RB165	B348	
RB166	B349	P136c
RB167	B354	P136d
RB168	B359	P136e
RB1001	B364	P143
RB1002	B365	
RB1003	B366	
RB1004		
RB1005		
RB1006		
RB1007		

TWENTY POUNDS
RB171	B227	P81
RB172	B230	P89
RB173	B243	P96
RB174	B318	
RB175	B319	} P134a
RB176	B328	
RB177	B329	} P134b
RB178	B350	P134c
RB180	B351	P134d
RB181	B355	P134e
RB182	B358	P141a
RB2001	B368	'B' Ream
RB2002	B367	
RB2003	B369	
RB2004	B370	
RB2005		
RB2006		

FIFTY POUNDS
RB191	B218	P82
RB192	B231	P90
RB193	B244	P97
RB194	B352	P138a
RB195	B356	P138b
RB196	B360	P138c
RB5001	B371	P145
RB5002		
RB5003		
RB5004		

ONE HUNDRED
RB201	B219	P83
RB202	B232	P91
RB203	B245	P98

TWO HUNDRED
RB220	B220	P84

FIVE HUNDRED
RB221	B221	P85
RB222	B233	P92
RB223	B246	P99

ONE THOUSAND
RB301	B222	P86
RB302	B234	P93
RB303	B247	P100

FIVE THOUSAND

FIFTEEN THOUSAND

COLLECTORS BANKNOTES · COMPARATIVE CATALOGUE NUMBERS